WHAT PEOPLE ARE SAYING ABOUT *YES!!!*

YES!!! That's the most dangerous word you could say. Once you say YES!!!, your world shifts. The question is, once you've said YES!!!, what then? Does everything work out smoothly? Are there no more struggles? How do I process my YES!!!? Glad you asked. In his book, *YES!!!*, my friend Chris Binion will unpack all that while illustrating it with great vulnerability and humor. Heaven is waiting for your YES!!!

—SAM CHAND
Leadership Consultant and author of *VOICES*

YES!!! hits hard—in the best way. The moment Chris's daughter sings in jail and the chaos literally stops? That was my aha moment. It's not just a story—it's a wake-up call. Obedience isn't clean or convenient; it's disruptive and powerful. Chris brings the fire with humor, grit, and soul. Every chapter dares you to stop playing it safe and say YES to God with everything you've got. If you're coasting, this book will jolt you back into purpose.

—MARTIJN VAN TILBORGH
Author, Speaker, and Co-Founder, AVAIL

YES!!!, is a timely and transformative message. With honesty, wisdom, and pastoral depth, Chris Binion masterfully reminds us that saying, "Yes!!!" to God isn't a one-time decision—it's a lifelong posture. Through compelling personal stories and biblical insight, this book offers more than encouragement; it provides a roadmap for obedient, faith-filled living in every season of life and leadership. Whether you're discerning your next step or recommitting to the one you've already taken, this book will equip you to respond to God's voice with confidence, courage, and conviction.

—DINO RIZZO
Executive Director, ARC

Chris Binion is an inspiring leader with a fun personality. His leadership style makes everyone want to connect with him and the vision God has put in his heart. With years of experience in corporate America and the church world, the wisdom Chris shares will help equip any leader. I'm honored to have his friendship and encouragement in my life. This book will motivate you to say one thing . . . "YES!!!"

— KODY HUGHES
Senior Pastor, The Heights Church

I've had the privilege of watching Pastor Chris Binion serve with integrity, humility, and an unwavering commitment to the Kingdom of God. In *YES!!!*, Chris opens his life with remarkable transparency, sharing the highs, the heartbreaks, and the holy moments that have shaped his journey. What makes this book so powerful is its honesty. Chris doesn't present polished theology or sanitized success stories. He offers something far more meaningful: a living testimony of what happens when ordinary people give God their full and unfiltered "yes." With moving vulnerability, he even shares deeply personal stories about his own family, reflections that showcase the redemptive power of God at work in everyday life. This is more than a memoir. It is a roadmap for any believer longing to walk in obedience, even when the path ahead is uncertain. Each chapter is rich with practical insight, Spirit-breathed encouragement, and real-life examples of faith in motion. Whether you are a young pastor, a seasoned leader, or someone wondering if God is still writing your story, this book will stir your faith, renew your hope, and remind you that even your smallest steps of obedience matter deeply to God. *YES!!!* is a timely, heartfelt, and deeply personal call to courageous surrender. I recommend it wholeheartedly.

—**ROB BAILEY**
Administrative Bishop
Texas Church of God

YES!!! is a powerful reminder that a simple "yes" to God can lead to extraordinary transformation. Chris Binion shares his journey with honesty, humor, and deep faith—calling each of us to step boldly into our kingdom assignment.

—**RYAN MOORE**
CEO, Builders International

Chris Binion is not only a gifted communicator and pastor—he's a friend whose "yes" to God has impacted countless lives. With humor, insight, and heart, this book will build your faith and challenge you to step into your own Kingdom assignment. I've seen firsthand how obedience like his can change everything.

—**PAUL ANDREW**
Executive Director of Pastors Collective

I know of no one more qualified to help you move forward in your Kingdom assignment than Chris Binion. *YES!!!* will not only teach you how to hear God's voice but will challenge and motivate you to live a life of purpose and fulfillment. When you live out your YES!!!, lives will be changed, including yours.

—**JUSTIN CHAMBERS**
Lead Pastor, New Song Church

Most of us do not know how much God could bless our lives, our families, and our future, if we would just say YES!!! to Him. Pastor Chris tells you plainly in this book how to say "yes" when God drops a word in your heart. You will laugh and cry at the stories he tells of those who have learned to follow God's voice. Read this book, put his counsel into practice, and you will see God respond to you too!

—PASTOR BOB ORDEMAN
Emeritus Pastor of International Christian Center

Chris Binion is one of the funniest, most joyful, faith-filled, and gracious people I've met in my life. He is a man of character, compassion, and love . . . so he's one of the special ones that God really cares about, right? The truth is that Chris had an encounter with God that has and is still shaping him into a reflection of God's character. In this funny and inspiring book, Chris opens his heart and gives us a followable model of what it looks like to say "yes" and follow God's heart and purpose so that we, too, can become a reflection of God's character. I hope you'll join him in this YES!!! Adventure—you'll never regret it!

—LAFE ANGEL
Lead Pastor
Grace Point Family Church

YES!!! Moving forward in his kingdom assignment has been a lifelong progressive journey for Chris Binion. I've known this prolific writer/author for many years. I've watched him navigate throughout this journey to follow the hand of God, which is evident in his life. Chris has been an inspiration and encourager to me, and what I know to be true is that this book is a true testament to his life as a husband, singer/songwriter, father, pastor, and friend. You'll never move forward without first saying YES!!! Apply these principles to your life, and you will move forward, too.

—**DR. H.W. "DUSTY" WILSON**
CEO, Spirit Sound Music Group

Chris Binion has written a book about one key that unlocks many doors—YES!!!—three little letters that actually spell "miracles" for anyone who dares to believe.

—**DR. TIM HILL**
Bishop, Tennessee Church of God

Chris Binion captures the enthusiasm and wonder of discovering how God can, and will, use you when you are a willing vessel. Saying "YES!!!" to God's direction empowers the believer, and Chris's testimony in this book proves the favor that comes upon those who obey the call and are willing to give God their "YES!!!"

—**BISHOP GARY LEWIS**
General Overseer, Church of God

Chris is an unforgettable individual with an indomitable personality! He is a gifted songwriter, singer, musician, preacher, teacher, entrepreneur, stand-up comic, and book writer. From my first encounter with him until now, he has not changed. His spiritual intimacy with the Lord, his life experiences, and his faith have taught him to always say "YES!!!" to God! The rest speaks for itself. He and Tracy have earned their stripes in life and in the ministry. They speak with authority out of their personal testimonies of God's amazing faithfulness and provision. This is a book written with personal application in mind and is also good for small group discussions. When you read it, you will "laugh a lot," you will "learn a lot," and you will "lean a lot" closer to the

Lord in becoming better prepared to say "YES!!!" to God's directives for your life!

—TERRY HARRIS
Missions Pastor, The Crossing Church

"YES!!!" There is no more impactful word in the English language than YES. It is the most "committal" heartfelt expression in one's life for covenant, calling, and purpose. In this book, my friend Chris Binion gives a masterful, God inspired guideline for every believer pursuing purpose and personal assignment in this incredible season of life.

—JAMIE TUTTLE
Lead Pastor, Dwelling Place Church International, Cleveland, Tennessee

Chris Binion has become one of my most cherished friends and confidants over the last eight years. When we planted our church, Chris was right there beside us, giving us some of the greatest encouragement. He has become a lifelong friend, yet we've known each other for less than a decade. Although Chris has faced a lot of adversity early on in his church planting endeavor, he never wavered from encouraging those around him. It is one of my greatest honors to endorse his new book, YES!!!, as the most prolific and profound encouragement a pastor, business owner, leader, and believer could ever read. I have no doubt that this book was written out of trials while learning to trust God through it all. Chris has experienced the power of an anointed YES!!!, and it is my belief and prayer that you can, too!

—SHANE TARPLEY
Lead Pastor, Verve Church

From time to time, an author captures the heart of the Christian faith in a way that both inspires and challenges readers. Chris Binion is one of those authors. His book isn't just about obedience to God's summons to fulfill our Kingdom assignment. He takes us to the heart of God to experience transformation from the inside out. Then, with a heart overflowing with love and power, we want to please the One who delights in us. With compelling stories, biblical insights, and his special brand of humor, God will use Chris's book to change your life. I'm sure of it.

—PAT SPRINGLE
Author and President of Baxter Press

Not only do I know Chris Binion, but he is my son. Nothing surprises me anymore when it comes to his heart for God and his constant pursuit of the things of God. From playing instruments, walking away from great jobs on different occasions to be a youth pastor, and now a founding pastor, from leading worship and even becoming an award-winning songwriter. I look back and see there was never a NO, it's always seemed to have been YES!!! So, why not write a book about it so others will be encouraged to say yes as well? I am a proud father with a great son, and I know his mother would have been so proud to share this YES!!! moment with him. Love you, son!

—GLEN BINION
Father of the author

We all love these three letters, Y.E.S. Unfortunately, some live in the two-letter world, N.O. As you read this book, you will be moved, encouraged, and empowered to change your NO to YES. Jesus gives us more YES!!! for living life. Allow Pastor Chris to take you on a journey to YES!!!

—DR. F. DOUGLAS BARKER
Friend of Jesus

Pastor Chris Binion doesn't just write about saying "yes" to God—he's lived it. This book is more than encouragement; it's a call to action. *YES!!!* will stir your faith, confront your comfort, and push you toward obedience—because the miracle is always on the other side of obedience. Read it ready. God's about to ask for your YES!!!

—**PASTOR NICK NEWMAN**
Lead Pastor, Propel Church
Founder, Selah Leaders

In a world full of distractions and detours, *YES!!!* by Chris Binion, this is a much-needed compass that points us back to the power of simple obedience. This heartwarming and humorous journey invites readers to consider the eternal impact of one courageous word—YES!!! When God whispered to Chris, "If you will continue to say 'YES!!!', I will do amazing things in you and through you," He set in motion a testimony of faith that continues to unfold in inspiring and transformational ways. Chris's storytelling is both relatable and profound, weaving biblical truth with personal experiences that will encourage anyone seeking clarity and direction in their spiritual walk. Whether you're reading alone or in a small group, this book is more than just words on a page—it's a practical tool for discovering your divine assignment and stepping into it with boldness. Say YES!!!—and watch what God will do.

—**ARCHBISHOP H. MICHAEL CHITWOOD, THD, DDIV.**
Founder and President, International
Congress of Churches and Ministers

Chris Binion is a powerful communicator and compassionate pastor who distills, in this book, decades of experience and wisdom. Gain a clearer vision for the pathway of choices that lie before you. Take the high road of holiness! Reach forward for the upward call of God. In this book, you're going to get Pastor Chris at his best.

—BOB SORGE
Author, Secrets of the Secret Place

Reading *YES!!!* feels like sitting down with a trusted friend who cheers you on to follow God wholeheartedly. Chris shares biblical truth, personal stories, and laugh-out-loud moments that inspire you to hear God more clearly—and obey Him immediately. With every chapter, you'll find yourself drawn closer to the heart of God and reminded that He still speaks, and that our greatest joy comes from saying YES!!! to Him. This book is honest, practical, and deeply encouraging. It will stir your faith, lift your spirit, and leave you excited to live a life of full surrender and adventure with God.

—MALLORY BASSHAM
Global Pastor, Gateway Church

My friend Chris Binion brings a powerful and practical word in this book. *YES!!!* is a call to trust God, push past the excuses, and step boldly into your Kingdom assignment. If you've been hesitating on what God's asked you to do, this book will give you the nudge and encouragement you need.

—GREG SURRATT
Seacoast Church
Founding Pastor

For someone like me, who is not a reader at all, I could not put this book down. I read *YES!!!* in less than one day (in a matter of hours). Pastor Chris Binion takes you through the simplicity of saying, "yes" to God with biblical applications for navigating and pushing past doubt, fear, and insecurities. Pastor Chris is a walking, living, breathing illustrated sermon of how your yes and moving forward open the doors for the impossible to become possible through God. He communicates this so well throughout this book. As you read *YES!!!*, you'll laugh, cry, and see that what God did for Pastor Chris, He can do for you when you say, "YES!!!" and move forward!

—CHRIS NEGRON
Campus Pastor
Encounter Church Quinlan

Chris Binion's *"YES!!!"* is a powerful and deeply personal call to courageous obedience. Through honest storytelling and biblical truth, Binion shows how a simple, consistent "yes" to God can transform a life and unlock a Kingdom assignment beyond what we could imagine. This book will challenge and inspire anyone ready to move forward in faith.

—ANDREW MIKEL EDWARDS
Campus Pastor
Elevation Church, Concord

This book is more than words on a page—it's the heartbeat of the man I love. I've had the honor of walking alongside my husband as he's chosen to say "YES!!!" again and again—not just to God's calling, but to the unknown, the uncomfortable, and the unseen. I've watched him wrestle, pray, trust, and move forward even when it didn't make sense. What you'll read in these pages isn't theory—it's truth lived out with deep faith and unwavering obedience.

If you've ever felt stuck, hesitant, or unsure of your purpose, this book will speak to you like a trusted friend. It will call you higher, stir your spirit, and remind you that your "YES!!!"

could unlock something far greater than you imagine. I know, because I've seen it firsthand in the one who wrote it.

—TRACY BINION
Co-Founder of Encounter Church
and The Pastor's Refuge
Wife of the author

For years, I have made two requests a part of my life prayers: first, that I would be able to hear God's voice clearly, and second, that I would have the courage to do whatever He says. Through this book, as well as his own life, Chris Binion has given me a huge dose of that courage.

—DAN OHLERKING
Children's Cup Executive Director

I have had the honor of walking beside Chris Binion in life and ministry for over thirty years—as colleagues, co-laborers, and brothers in the faith. Through seasons of great joy and deep challenges, Chris has remained a man of unshakable integrity, transparent vulnerability, and unwavering commitment to God's call. In *YES!!!*, Chris opens the door to his own personal journey with raw honesty, humor, and Spirit-breathed wisdom. With every page, he invites readers to say "yes" to God—not just once, but continually—as a posture of purpose, surrender, and destiny. His stories are refreshingly real, his teaching is deeply rooted in Scripture, and his voice resonates with the authenticity of a man who has lived what he writes. This is more than a book—it's a divine invitation. If you are seeking clarity in your calling, courage for your assignment, or fresh faith for the next step, this book will equip and encourage you to move forward in obedience. YES!!! is a timely word for a generation searching for direction and significance in the

Kingdom of God. Say "YES!!!" to reading this book and move forward. It just might change everything.

—**KEITH DUNCAN**
His Call Ministries, Inc.

I've said "yes" way too many times to people and programs, but never as much to God. Saying yes to people has broken my heart. Saying yes to programs has worn me down to a nub. However, saying yes to God has healed my heart and built me up into an oak. Pastor Binion is inviting you and me into a trust lifestyle with God that will never disappoint, for in the context of saying yes to God, all things indeed work together for the good (Romans 8:28). With wit and wisdom, Chris nurtures trusting God with all your heart, not leaning on your own understanding and saying yes to His will which will be the right path to take (Proverbs 3:5-6). You're in for a fun and fruitful read. After reading this book, I'm confident you'll agree with Chris: "All of God's blessings are yours if you'll say, 'Yes!!!' to Him."

—**DR. STEVE HALL**
Associate Professor of Pastoral Ministry at Lee University
Executive Director of MinistryOasis.com

YES!!!

Copyright © 2025 by Chris Binion

Published by AVAIL

All rights reserved. No portion of this book may be reproduced, stored in a retrieval system, or transmitted in any form or by any means—electronic, mechanical, photocopy, recording, scanning, or other—except for brief quotations in critical reviews or articles, without prior written permission of the author.

Unless otherwise specified, all Scripture quotations are taken from the New King James Version®. Copyright © 1982 by Thomas Nelson. Used by permission. All rights reserved. | Scripture quotations marked NIV are taken from the Holy Bible, New International Version®, NIV®. Copyright © 1973, 1978, 1984, 2011 by Biblica, Inc.™ Used by permission of Zondervan. All rights reserved worldwide. www.zondervan.com. The "NIV" and "New International Version" are trademarks registered in the United States Patent and Trademark Office by Biblica, Inc.™

For foreign and subsidiary rights, contact the author.

Cover design by: Sara Young
Cover photo by: Keith Betters

ISBN: 978-1-964794-94-5   1 2 3 4 5 6 7 8 9 10

Printed in the United States of America

YES!!!

MOVING FORWARD IN YOUR KINGDOM ASSIGNMENT

CHRIS BINION

CONTENTS

Acknowledgments. xxv

INTRODUCTION 27

CHAPTER 1. **YOUR ENCOUNTER**. 29

CHAPTER 2. **YOUR "YES!!!" CHANGES EVERYTHING** 57

CHAPTER 3. **THE JOURNEY OF SURPRISES** 83

CHAPTER 4. **OBSTACLES ARE OPPORTUNITIES** 109

CHAPTER 5. **THE PROMISE IS A PROCESS** 131

CHAPTER 6. **BELIEVING FOR THE UNBELIEVABLE** 151

CHAPTER 7. **ON THE OTHER SIDE OF OBEDIENCE**. 183

CHAPTER 8. **YOU HAVE MY "YES!!!"** 197

USING *YES!!!* IN SMALL GROUPS AND CLASSES 227

ABOUT THE AUTHOR. 233

ACKNOWLEDGMENTS

I'm grateful to the many people who have shaped me. This message—the message of YES!!!—was born from their influence. To my parents, who have always invested in me and the Kingdom assignments God has called me to carry.

To my wife of almost thirty-six years, you have been my constant companion, that one person who believed in me so much that she followed when it was hard and lovingly pushed me forward with her unwavering words of affirmation.

To my children, Chase and Haley—my heart is full knowing we get to do ministry together. I love you tremendously.

To my Encounter Church family across all three campuses—thank you for your resounding "YES!!!" To all my friends and peers who have patiently listened to my testimonies on repeat, like a broken record endlessly skipping over moments that felt extremely braggadocious—my apologies . . . again! But transparently, your friendship has been a safe space for me to share openly. While some might view those moments competitively, you helped me celebrate them for what they truly are—"I can't believe this happened!" moments of God's goodness.

To AVAIL and the entire team who did all the behind-the-scenes directing and publishing.

To my writing partner, Pat Springle, who laughed with me in every interview, endured the emotional moments as I shared the hard things, helped me shape the message, clarify the heart, and put words to what once lived only in my spirit . . . I am grateful. Thank you!

INTRODUCTION

This book is all about saying "YES!!!" But not just any YES ... this is the type of YES that creates forward movement. This is your "YES!!!", that moment where you decide that you've been stagnant long enough. That moment when you finally take steps to move forward because God has turned your fear into faith and your faith into favor. This is literally the moment where you realize the power of your "YES!!!" and that you're the only one that can give it! ARE YOU READY???

CHAPTER ONE

YOUR ENCOUNTER

"Eye has not seen, nor ear heard, Nor have entered into the heart of man The things which God has prepared for those who love Him."
—1 Corinthians 2:9

"One encounter with God can change everything!" That's the first message people see when they walk through the doors of the church. My wife, Tracy, and I believe it so much that we named the church "Encounter Church." We want people to be inspired from the first moment they interact with us, but along with the inspiration is a warning: the little word "can." God takes the initiative to touch the hearts of people, but as you know, some respond in grateful faith and dedicated action, but others say, in effect, "Thanks, but no thanks," or "I'll wait until tomorrow," or "I'd love to, but . . ." To experience a mind-expanding, heart-filling encounter with God, we have to say, "Yes!" . . .

and mean it. Our faith-filled response starts with a single encounter, but it can become the habit of a lifetime.

Let me describe my encounters with God.

A BETTER "YES!!!"

I trusted in Jesus when I was a little boy, but when I got into high school, I started doing "Chris things" instead of "Christ things." My father was a pastor, so I was always in church. I played the drums and served in many other ways. My body was in the building, but my heart was somewhere else. I told people I had a drug problem: my parents "drug" me to church every time the doors were open.

When I was sixteen, I was in church one Sunday night when the Spirit was moving. I looked around the room and saw people pouring their hearts out in worship and repentance, but I felt nothing . . . absolutely nothing, and it scared me. I wondered if I'd blasphemed the Holy Spirit, but I'd never heard any pastor explain that concept. I heard them talk about sin and hell so often that I was sure the only thing they didn't preach against was fresh air.

I prayed, "Lord, I don't read my Bible, and I don't pray, but when I'm in church, I expect to feel Your presence." I knew that didn't make sense. I walked down to the altar, and I remembered the story of Jacob wrestling with the angel (or maybe the pre-incarnate Christ) and saying, "I won't let go until You bless me!" (Genesis 32:26, author paraphrase)

I stayed at the altar for an hour, waiting for the touch of the Spirit, but . . . silence. Older people came to lay hands on me and pray. One advised me, "Let go," and another said, "Hold on." Still . . . nothing.

Finally, I prayed, "Lord, I'm so sorry for neglecting You!" I wasn't afraid I was going to hell, but I was deeply saddened that I wasn't emotionally connected to the One who loved me enough to die for me. In that moment, the Lord met me, comforted me, and drew me close. I was so happy!

That day was a different kind of "Yes!" In the past, I'd raised my hand to say that I wanted God to rescue me from hell, but fire insurance didn't thrill me, capture me, inspire me, or empower me. Instead of thinking nonstop about how to play Nintendo better, I started considering how to use every moment of every day to honor Jesus.

While in high school, I began considering who I might date and marry. I didn't want to mess around. I wanted God to show me who He wanted me to marry—and get 'er done! I had a date with an attractive girl, but it didn't click. I thought, *Okay, tried that. No more.* I wanted God to give me a wife as a good gift. A gift isn't something you have to search for. It's given to you . . . you just need to receive it.

I met Tracy and then began a ministerial internship program. She helped me study. I graduated when I was eighteen. Our families were polar opposites. My parents loved each other, and their marriage was strong. Tracy's family was more than broken; it was shattered. We seemed like a pretty good fit.

I was serving in my father's church. One day, Dad told me that the guy who was leading a class for little kids needed "an extended Sabbath," and he asked me to step in. There were only two kids that first week, but before long, forty children attended regularly. The guy told Dad that he was ready to come back and lead the class. It was God's class, not mine, so I was more than willing to let him have it. In a few weeks, it was down to two or three again. He told Dad he needed another Sabbath, so he handed the class to me again. (I think he needed more than a Sabbath!)

Later, Dad asked me to help with worship. I already played the drums, so helping was easy. I learned to play the bass guitar and the piano. Then, he asked me to lead worship.

I graduated from high school, and Tracy and I got married on June 10, 1989. I didn't have a job. (How crazy is that?) She said, "I'm not worried. I've seen your father's work ethic, and he'll *make* you get a job so you can take care of me."

I told the Lord, "I want to work Monday through Friday. I don't want to work on the weekends, so I'll be free to serve in the church." Somebody suggested that "bankers' hours" fit my requirements, so I called one of the banks in town to ask if they had any openings for tellers.

The HR person asked, "Do you have experience as a teller?"

I answered, "No, but I'm a quick learner." She wasn't convinced.

When I got the same answer at another bank, I asked, "If you need experienced tellers but can't find them, how can I get training so you can hire me?"

I thought it was a great question, but he responded, "Sorry. That won't work."

I called Sunbelt National Mortgage Company and was directed to their HR department and Mrs. Johnson. I thought, *Here we go again.* I introduced myself, explained that I was newly married, and promised to be a hard worker. I explained, "I'd like a job, and I'm open to anything you have available. I'll mop floors, wash windows, vacuum . . . whatever you need." I'm glad they didn't take me up on that because the truth be known, my mom made my bed until I moved out at nineteen when Tracy and I were married, and she can confirm my cleaning skillset was definitely lacking.

Mrs. Johnson was sweet, but she told me, "I appreciate your willingness, but we just filled the only position we had open. It was in the mail room." She paused for a second, and then said, "Why don't you call me in a couple of weeks to see if anything opens up?"

It was a ray of light—a faint one, but it was the best one so far. I didn't wait two weeks. I called her a week later. She said she still didn't have anything open, but she suggested I call back. I called three days later, and she again said there were no slots available. She said, "I appreciate your tenacity. Call me again in a week."

The next Monday morning, when the doors opened, I walked in wearing a suit and tie. I sat in the lobby, and when someone came out and asked who my appointment was with, I said, "I don't have an appointment, but I'm here to see Mrs. Johnson in HR. I'll wait until she's available."

When she was told I was in the lobby, she came out to see me. I told her, "I know I don't have an appointment, but I'm so glad to see you." We went back to her office. I told her again that I was eager to be hired (as if she couldn't tell).

She smiled and shook her head. "We haven't had any new openings, but the person we hired for the mail room didn't work out. Would you like the job?"

I almost jumped out of my chair. "Yes! I'll start today!"

Mrs. Johnson laughed. "You can't start today. We have to take you through our hiring process. If things work out—and I'm sure they will—you can start next week."

She knew I'd said, "Yes!" before I heard the question.

In five years at Sunbelt, I was promoted a couple of times—from the mailroom to a payoff specialist who handles the paperwork to release liens on houses.

I appreciated the opportunity to work at the mortgage company, but in my heart, I knew something was missing. I told the Lord that I wanted to be great in His kingdom. I didn't care if anyone saw me serve, but I wanted to minister in a way that pleased God and filled my heart.

I sensed the Spirit tell me to go to a camp meeting in Weatherford, Texas. The next morning, I drove to Weatherford. I sat in the choir area for the morning session. Pastor Ole Olds preached. I couldn't tell you what he spoke about, but I became increasingly convicted by the Spirit. I told God, "I'll do anything, I'll go anywhere, and I'll serve in any way You choose. I'm Yours. If You want me to be a mortgage banker, I want to be the best I can be. If You want me to go into vocational ministry, show me." I went to the altar to pray. I guess a lot of people thought I was trusting in Jesus for salvation because several of them put their hands on my shoulders and prayed, "Save him, Lord."

When the session was over, a man asked me to go to lunch with him and a couple of others who happened to be pastors. One of them, William Carnley, pastored a church in Wichita Falls, Texas. He explained that his church needed to hire a youth pastor, and he invited me to send him my resume if I was interested.

I sent Pastor Carnley my resume, but I didn't tell Tracy about any of this. Things got a lot dicier when the Spirit told me, "Now, quit your job."

What? Hold up, Jesus! I was sure that was some bad nachos I'd eaten, not the Holy Spirit, but I sensed Him say, "Give your boss your two-week notice."

So far, I'd said, "Yes!" at every point, but this time, I said, "Um, yeah, kind of." I gave my boss a one-month notice. I concluded that this would give me enough time to find another job if the Lord didn't come through with this job as a youth pastor. I still hadn't told Tracy a thing.

Two weeks later, I got cold feet. I knocked on my boss's door and asked, "Hey, is there any chance I can take that one-month notice back and stay here?"

He shook his head. "No, sorry. We've already hired someone, and we're using the next two weeks to train him to take your spot."

Now I *had to* tell Tracy.

I don't think I slept more than a few minutes each night for the next week. With one more week to go at Sunbelt, it was time. For some reason, Tracy and I bought a ping-pong table for our little apartment. After supper, I asked, "Hey, do you want to play ping pong?"

She said, "Sure."

"You stand on that side near the sliding glass door to outside." I stood near the phone (the old kind with cords and wires and everything). It was close to the front door, so if she attacked me, I could run out the door and jump in the car before she could catch me. I'm not very fast, but I thought I could outrun her that far.

I stammered, "Baby doll, there's something I need to tell you."

She looked puzzled and asked, "Is everything okay?"

Before I could speak another syllable, the phone rang. I jumped for it. "Let me get this, and then I'll tell you."

It was Pastor Carnley. "Brother Chris, the church board met tonight and picked you out of thirteen applicants to be the new youth pastor. You can start next week." Thirteen! I thought I was the only one. If I had known that I would never have given my notice at Sunbelt.

I responded, "Thank you, Pastor. I can't wait to join you."

How do you spell relief? J-O-B.

I hung up the phone and looked across the ping-pong table at a very curious woman. I was thrilled that I didn't have to tell her I was unemployed, but now I had to explain that we were moving in the next few days!

I started my spiel again: "Baby girl, I have something really good to tell you." I told her the story about the camp meeting, the lunch with the pastors, the invitation to send my resume to Pastor Carnley, turning in my notice, and the call I just received.

From the look on Tracy's face, I discerned that she didn't think this was "really good" news.

She chewed on me a bit: "Chris, we're married. You have to tell me these things!"

Of course, she was right, but I'd been a coward. I didn't want her to think I'd lost my mind. (In case you're wondering, this is not in the "Best Practices" section of the marriage how-to manual.)

When I got to Wichita Falls, I felt totally inadequate. I'd never been a youth pastor. I'd led worship and a kids' class, but I knew someone who knew what they needed: the Lord. I went to the youth office, knelt down, and asked God to give me wisdom, power, and love for these kids. I thought about Jeremiah being a young man when God called him. I told God I'd do whatever He told me to do. The Lord directed me to ask if we could use the sign in front of the church. I heard over and over, "Get sodas. Get coolers." I sensed God wanted me to buy something besides Coke and Dr. Pepper. I heard, "Orange, grape, and red."

I called a local grocery store and spoke to the manager. I said, "I'm the new youth pastor at the church down the street, and we need some sodas for our teenagers: orange, grape, and red." I explained that we were giving the sodas to students on their way home from school.

He told me, "Come get them every week. They're free. I'll throw in as much ice as you need." People in the church donated three big coolers, so we were all set.

On the next Wednesday afternoon, I put on the sign: "What would God say to Madonna?"

Adults in the church may have responded, "Well, God would tell her she's going to hell!" But it gave me the opportunity to explain that God's grace extends to every person on the planet—those who feel overlooked and abandoned, and those who are in the limelight. When kids came by, we let them pick a drink, and we gave them a handout inviting them to our youth group that night.

The next Wednesday afternoon, more kids came for sodas. The sign read, "Who is God?"

By the third Wednesday, kids ran to the church to get sodas. The sign that week said, "How Does it Feel to Die?"

We didn't have music on Wednesday nights. I prepared messages I thought would capture their hearts. One week, I taught James 3 about the tongue, and I brought a pig's tongue. They were grossed out, but they loved it. (I used it to lick a few of their arms and faces.)

On the fourth Wednesday, we ran out of sodas really fast. The sign read, "Who Cares?"

In four weeks, the youth group grew from six to ninety-two students. In a few more weeks, 120 showed up, so we had two services on Wednesday nights. Tracy drove a van to pick up the kids who were too young to drive. I told her not to put twenty-two kids in a fifteen-passenger van, but she explained, "If they want to come, I'm picking them up!"

This "Yes!" was a big one, but it wasn't the last one. When Joshua led God's people across the Jordan at flood stage, his "Yes!" was an echo of Moses leading the people through the Red Sea forty years earlier. One "Yes!" encourages the next one, and I was about to see this principle in action.

The youth group grew so large that we couldn't fit in the room, even with two services on Wednesday nights. Some of the leaders in the church felt uncomfortable with all the kids coming, so they decided to downsize—they informed me that my services were no longer needed. I was devastated. I prayed, "Lord, I've said 'Yes!' to You. How can this happen?"

I wanted to go to Lee College in Cleveland, Tennessee, but Tracy and I had two children, so I needed a job to support my family. We packed up our things and got ready to leave, but I forgot to pack our telephone. I ran back into the parsonage to get it, and when I was about to unplug it from the wall, it rang. I answered, and the voice on the line said, "Chris, this is Terry Harris. I pastor a church in Chattanooga. I've heard some great things about you. We need to hire a youth pastor, and I want to interview you if you're interested."

I explained that I planned to attend Lee College, and he shared, "If you're our full-time youth pastor, I'll make sure you get to attend Lee."

I put my back against the bare wall and started bawling. After the conversation, I unplugged the phone and carried it to the truck. Tracy saw that I'd been crying. She thought I was sad because we were leaving, but I was thrilled that God had seen my heart and opened a door for me. We had an interim stop at North Main Church of God in Weatherford, Texas, where Ted and Charlene Gray were pastoring. We were given the opportunity to not only lead the youth but also the worship experience on Sundays. After a few short months, we headed for Terry Harris's church in Chattanooga. The youth ministry there grew from sixteen to eighty-five in just over a year.

At each point, I sensed God's clear directive to go to my next kingdom assignment, and each time, I said "Yes!"

God called us to Pastor Bob Collins' church in Newport News, Virginia, and we experienced an incredible move of God. The Lord led the church into a God encounter where services would become nightly—each night of the week except Saturday and three on Sunday . . . for sixteen weeks. At the beginning, we had twenty-six students. When we left, there were over 400. We had five staff members and our own building, four miles from the church. Again, God said, "I told you that if you'll say 'Yes!', I'll do amazing things in you and through you."

When we'd been there for almost six-and-a-half years, I sensed God redirecting me to go into administration. It didn't make sense, but I said, "Yes!" I told Pastor Bob, and both of us cried. He said, "I don't want you to leave."

I blubbered, "I don't either!" I explained, "But Pastor, I can't take money to fulfill a vision where God hasn't called me. That's stealing."

Somewhere along the way, I'd learned my lesson about keeping Tracy informed. When I explained what I heard God tell me to do, she announced, "He told me the same thing."

Whew! That was sweet.

We moved back to Texas, and I looked for a job in administration. My father had started a business in two-way radio sales. I went to work for him, but it wasn't administration. A friend asked me to join him at Whitehall Jewelers. I told him I had absolutely no background in jewelry (unless you count belts), but he pleaded with me to work during the Christmas season to see how I liked it.

I must have done pretty well because the company was shocked that I had no returns. They offered me a job as a store manager. I appreciated the offer, but I didn't sense it was right for me. A few days later, another friend called to offer me an opportunity to apply for a job at Wells Fargo. I was there for eight years and got eight promotions. At the end of that time, I was forty-three years old and had a role covering five states in their home equity products division.

Wells Fargo bought Wachovia and put me in a lead role to help their executives and staff with our structures and systems, regarding credit. God had given me a prime administrative role in the second-largest bank in America.

The journey had been circuitous, but I'd learned a lot about both business and ministry. I would have never chosen this route, but I'd said, "Yes!" each time the Lord gave me directions.

THE CHURCH PLANTING "YES!!!"

I never wanted to be a pastor. I was working at Wells Fargo and was fully engaged in serving our pastor, but it never crossed my mind that I could (or should) have that role. I was perfectly comfortable in the background. God used me as a student ministry consultant and in leading worship. Whenever Tracy and I were asked to serve, we said, "Yes!"

One Sunday morning, the Spirit moved as we sang "Forever" by Kari Jobe. In one part of the song, it describes Jesus's resurrection and addresses death itself:

> *Forever, He is glorified*
> *Forever, He is lifted high.*[1]

I looked around the room and saw some people standing with their arms raised in praise; some were kneeling and weeping; and others sat and sang their hearts out. It was powerful and beautiful. When the song ended, the video announcements abruptly began playing. It was like he had scratched the needle on a Mozart album—totally out of place. The agenda of man had pushed out the sublime worship of God. In one sense, I understood what was happening. Our church had multiple services, so we had to end worship on time and get people out so we could start the next service. But it didn't seem right to me.

---

[1] Kari Jobe, vocalist, "Forever" by Brian Johnson, Joel Taylor, Jenn Johnson, Gabriel Wilson, Christa Black Gifford, and Kari Brooke Jobe, *Majestic*, February 18, 2014, track 6 on Majestic, Sparrow Records.

When we walked out to the parking lot and got in the car, Tracy looked at me and asked, "Are you okay?"

I never want to be disloyal to our pastor or the church, so I tried to look like a high-stakes poker player trying to bluff, but I told her, "No, I don't think I am."

I expected her to console me, but without missing a beat, she announced, "You know, the only way we can have the kind of church we want is to plant one."

Huh? I looked at her and said, "I rebuke you, devil!" A second later, I asked, "What do you want for lunch?" I thought the conversation about starting a church was over, zipped up, and gone forever.

But the idea wouldn't go away. It was like a tiny pebble in your shoe that you feel every time you take a step. I couldn't stop thinking about planting a church. I even dreamed about it! (I was kind of upset with Tracy for mentioning it.) I decided to run the idea past a couple of wise friends. Both were intrigued, and one of them said, "If you do it, I'll give you $500 a month for the first year."

I didn't know how to respond. I was thankful for his generosity, but it looked like God was already providing for a dream I was trying hard to ignore. One of my friends told me, "Chris, you need to talk to the people at ARC, the Association of Related Churches. They help people plant churches."

I looked up ARC and saw they had a conference coming in the fall of 2016, which was only a couple of months away. Patrick Wooten, another pastor I knew, offered to pay the expenses for Tracy and me to attend, and I knew this was it: God was in this crazy idea. I asked Tracy, "What do we have to lose?" She smiled, so I filled in the blanks, "The worst-case scenario is that we'll fail, but at least we will have tried."

I soon realized I had been saying "Yes!" to each prompting of the Spirit, even though each step surfaced even more questions. Continuing to say "Yes!" was all God was asking of me. I didn't need the answers . . . yet.

We registered for the conference in Birmingham and filled out forms so we could have a formal interview there. We watched their videos so we'd know what we were getting into and paid the $99 fee for the interview and vetting process. They asked us to create a video to share why we wanted to plant a church. I pulled out my phone, hit video record, and introduced Tracy and me. I said, "You asked us to tell you why we want to be part of ARC, but to be honest, I don't know that we do. We don't know you, and you don't know us. We'll know a lot more about each other when we meet at the conference." Not exactly ready for prime time, huh?

At the conference, we met many wonderful people. I was really impressed with them. One day after one of the sessions, Tracy and I walked to the elevator to go to our room, and we noticed a man behind us. He got on the elevator, too. Tracy joked with him, "Are you following us?"

He laughed and asked why we were at the hotel. Tracy told him we were attending the ARC conference to see if we might be a good fit to plant a church. He was gracious and polite. As he got off the elevator on his floor, he turned and told us, "I hope you have a great time."

The next afternoon, the speaker at the final session walked onto the stage. It was that guy, Scott Hornsby! Tracy looked at me and whispered, "Chris, they're *definitely* not going to let us in now!"

Our vetting meeting was scheduled an hour after the last session was over. We followed the directions to the meeting place and nervously went in. We let them know we were there and sat down to wait our turn to be interviewed. A few minutes later, an ARC host led us back to the room for the interview, and surprise—there was Scott Hornsby! The interview included another couple who interviewed us, but the guy from the elevator had me mesmerized. During our discussion, Scott and the other couple patiently answered all our questions. Scott asked, "When are you going to leave your job in banking so you can be a full-time pastor?"

"Never!" I blurted out. "The church can't afford to pay me what the bank does.

I don't want to go broke, and I'm too fluffy to go hungry, so I'm sticking with the bank."

We all laughed. I had no idea what they were thinking, and then Scott said, "Well, we want you to be one of us, an ARC church planter."

Oh man, this was getting really real really fast!

We planned to start the church in January, but we soon realized that wasn't realistic, so we delayed the grand opening until September.

If you've ever been part of a church plant, you know that you need a "church in a box," all the setup components in storage containers so you (and a couple of dozen faithful people) can unload the trailer early Sunday morning, set up lights, sound, chairs, and everything else, and then pack it up after the service and take it back to the storage area. One of my "yeses" was a bit reluctant. I sensed the Lord tell me to get on Facebook Marketplace. I had no idea why I needed to do that, but it dawned on me that I might find everything we needed there. I found a guy in Georgetown, Texas, near Austin, who had the cases we needed. When I called, he said he wanted $3,500 for them. I swallowed hard and asked, "How about $2,000?"

He explained, "I don't know if you need them, but there's a podium and a keyboard already in one of the cases."

It was the podium and keyboard I was planning to buy! I told him, "We'll do the $3,500."

We had nice cases, but we didn't have a trailer to haul them. I called somebody who called somebody else, and eventually, God led me to a company that offered to sell me a trailer at a ridiculously low price. It was so low that I asked, "Uh, is it in good shape?"

The man answered, "It's brand new."

When I arrived to get it, I saw the company's name on a sign at the entrance: Salvation Trailers. Perfect.

ARC had a program of matching funds: church plants that raised $50,000 would receive that amount from the organization. I had no idea where that much money would come from, but people started giving us money, and we hit that goal. We had over $100,000 in seed money to launch the church.

Encounter Church is a product of the thousands of times when people, including me, said, "Yes!" to God.

THE ROCK ON WHICH WE STAND

Many people have walked forward during an invitation, thrown their stick in the fire at youth camp, prayed a sincere prayer with a friend or pastor, or indicated in some other way that the Spirit of God has touched their hearts and revealed the gospel of grace found only in Jesus's death, burial, and resurrection . . . but there was a flaw in their grasp of what happened at that moment. They saw their decision as fire insurance. Yes, it's that, but it's far, far more.

Jesus is "the Lord, Jesus Christ." *Christ* isn't His last name. Christ is the Greek word for the Jewish Messiah—the One God promised Abraham would be a blessing to the entire world, the One the prophet Isaiah predicted would be the ultimate Lamb sacrificed for our sins, and the One who would rule as King over His people and the whole world.

> **THE WORLD VALUES ACCLAIM, POWER, AND WEALTH, BUT JESUS'S KINGDOM TURNS ALL THIS ON ITS HEAD.**

The term "Lord" had much more significance in the first centuries of the church than today. In the Roman Empire, people were commanded to say, "Caesar is lord." If they didn't, they were punished until the pain persuaded them to change their minds . . . or they were executed. When Christians said, "Jesus is Lord," it was a radical, subversive, courageous declaration that they were willing to obey Jesus and follow Him no matter the price they'd have to pay. And many paid the ultimate price. For instance, in the year 112, Pliny the Younger was governor of Bithynia (in modern Turkey). Christians were brought before him on unspecified charges. These people seemed harmless to him, but they refused to say, "Caesar is lord." That was enough of a crime. He demanded they recant, and he warned that if they refused, they'd be killed. Still, he was unsure if this was the right course, so he wrote a letter to his friend, Emperor Trajan, who replied that executing the unrepentant Christians was the right thing to do.[2]

My point (in case you missed it) is that becoming a Christian—then and today—is a radical reorientation of our lives: our purpose, our desires, our hopes, our words, our actions, and our relationships. When we acknowledge Jesus is our Lord, we die to our old, self-centered life and live for Him, transformed from the inside out by the power of the Holy Spirit. At our baptism, we went under the waters that symbolized the death and burial of Jesus. All our sins—past, present, and future—were paid for by His death, so we're completely forgiven. Coming out of the water symbolizes Christ's resurrection to new life: a life reoriented to Christ

---
[2] Translated by William Whiston from *The Works of Josephus* (Peabody, MA: Hendrickson Publishers, 1987), https://www.pbs.org/wgbh/pages/frontline/shows/religion/maps/primary/pliny.html.

and His agenda. When He is our Lord, we live every day with the primary purpose of knowing Him more intimately, trusting Him more fully, and representing Him in every thought, word, and deed. Of course, we fall short. Our old nature is still present, and "the enemy of our souls" still tries to confuse and distract us, but we have the assurances that in Christ, there's no condemnation (Romans 8:1), and in Him, there's no separation from His love (Romans 8:38-39).

The word "gospel" means good news. When a new Roman emperor was crowned, the word went out, announcing the good news of the coronation. The New Testament writers picked up this concept and used it to announce a new king, but He was a King unlike any other. He was (and is) the crucified and risen King who has launched an upside-down kingdom. The world values acclaim, power, and wealth, but Jesus's kingdom turns all this on its head: To gain status, be a humble servant; to acquire power, acknowledge your weakness; to be truly rich, to be extraordinarily generous; to be right with God, admit you're a deeply flawed sinner in need of cleansing and restoration. Our King isn't like any other king who ever lived. When we're overwhelmed and thrilled that Jesus is both Savior *and* Lord, our encounter with Him *does* change everything!

YOUR "YES!!!"

Researchers have shown that we're creatures of habits. Our brains are wired to follow a time-tested and predictable pattern of thought and behavior. Many of us have a deeply grooved brain pattern of saying, "Maybe," "I'll think about it," or "Probably not" when God speaks to us. We've said it so often that it's become instinctive . . . and hard to change. But thank God, His Spirit, His Word, and His body of believers can reshape the very neurons in our brains, changing them to conform to a new pattern of saying, "Yes!" when God speaks to us.

Thankfully, I had a lot of positive reinforcement in my childhood. My parents gave me a leg up by loving me, protecting me, and encouraging me to follow God. Like everyone else, I had hurdles to overcome—the lure of the world, the lusts of the flesh, and the whispers and shouts of the enemy. But I learned early to respond in faith (most of the time) when God speaks to me, and I'm very grateful. My point is that no matter your background, God can work in your brain and heart to develop a new habit of repeatedly (but not perfectly) saying "Yes!" to Him.

> **GOD WANTS TO BLESS US FAR MORE THAN WE WANT HIS BLESSING.**

What does a "Yes!" look like? Thanks for asking. Professor and author Os Guinness defines God's invitation as "the truth that God calls us to himself so decisively that everything we are, everything we do, and everything we have is invested with a special devotion and dynamism lived out as a response to his summons and service."[3]

Who is the One who calls us? Guinness explains, "God calls people to himself, but this call is no casual suggestion. He is so awe-inspiring and his summons so commanding that only one response is appropriate—a response as total and universal as the authority of the Caller."[4]

We're naturally wary of someone we don't trust. When they tell us to do something, we delay, deny, or distract ourselves to avoid responding. But God is supremely trustworthy. He has proven Himself in many ways, but most assuredly through the cross and the resurrection of Jesus. The cross tells us of God's love and forgiveness. Jesus loves us so much that He paid the price we deserved to pay and gives us the honor He deserves from the Father. And the resurrection tells us about God's awesome power. God wants to bless us far more than we want His blessing. He delights in us and wants the very best for us. Certainly, His path for us can be confusing, but we never need to doubt His intentions. When Paul wrote to the Christians in Corinth, they weren't exactly stellar in their behavior. They argued, were jealous, and divided into competing factions (sounds

---

[3] Os Guinness, *The Call: Finding and Fulfilling the Central Purpose of Your Life* (Nashville, TN: Thomas Nelson, 2003), 4.
[4] Guiness, *The Call*, p. 30.

familiar, doesn't it?). But Paul looked beyond their pettiness to give them a stunning picture of God's purposes for them:

> *"Eye has not seen, nor ear heard,*
> *Nor have entered into the heart of man*
> *The things which God has prepared*
> *for those who love Him."*
> **—1 Corinthians 2:9**

All of God's blessings are yours if you'll say, "Yes!" to Him—not once or twice, but continually as a beloved child responds to a loving parent and a valued servant follows the lead of a gracious king.

At the end of each chapter, you'll find some questions designed to stimulate your thinking and prod deeper discussions with your spouse, friends, and small group. Don't rush through these. There are no points for speed! Ask God to open your heart to His goodness and greatness and say, "Yes!" to Him.

THINK ABOUT IT

CHAPTER 1

> **!** Look again at 1 Corinthians 2:9. What are some ways you can tell if you really believe God is this good and generous?

> **!** Describe a time when God gave you instructions and you said, "Yes!" What did God do (or not do) after that?

> **!** Describe a time when you used excuses to avoid saying, "Yes!" What were the consequences?

> **!** What promises in the Bible encourage you to trust God enough to say, "Yes!" to Him?

> **!** Explain how mental habits shape our responses to God at any given moment.

> **!** What do you hope to get out of this book?

CHAPTER TWO

YOUR "YES!!!" CHANGES EVERYTHING

For all the promises of God in Him are *Yes, and in Him Amen, to the glory of God through us.*
—**2 Corinthians 1:20**

Paul's second letter to the church in Corinth is both gritty and hopeful. Between his first letter and the second one, a lot of difficult things had happened. I mentioned that the Christians in the city were jealous and divisive. Well, things hadn't gotten any better! They had turned against Paul, and now, he had to defend his role as an apostle because they were dumping him. And besides, Paul had suffered so severely that he thought he was going to die. In the opening section of the letter, he explained:

> *For we do not want you to be ignorant, brethren, of our trouble which came to us in Asia: that we were burdened beyond measure, above strength, so that we despaired even of life. Yes, we had the sentence of death in ourselves, that we should not trust in ourselves but in God who raises the dead, who delivered us from so great a death, and does deliver us.*
> **—2 Corinthians 1:8-10**

Arrest and imprisonment have a way of changing a person's plans, and the Corinthians were upset that Paul hadn't come when he intended to visit them again. It was like they were saying, "You can make travel reservations in prison, can't you?" They accused him of going back on his word. That's the context for Paul's proclamation:

> *Therefore, when I was planning this, did I do it lightly? Or the things I plan, do I plan according to the flesh, that with me there should be Yes, Yes, and No, No? But as God is faithful, our word to you was not Yes and No. For the Son of God, Jesus Christ, who was preached among you by us—by me, Silvanus, and Timothy—was not Yes and No, but in Him was Yes. For all the promises of God in Him are Yes, and in Him Amen, to the glory of God through us.*
> **—2 Corinthians 1:17-20**

My point (or, more importantly, Paul's point) is that our "Yes!" to Jesus is often in the middle of heartache, confusion, roadblocks, and detours. Paul concludes his explanation with profound hope: "Now He who establishes us with you in Christ and has anointed us *is* God, who also has sealed us and given us the Spirit in our hearts as a guarantee" (2 Corinthians 1:21-22). We don't only say "Yes!" when the road ahead is smooth and beautiful; we also say "Yes!" when it seems everything is falling apart.

When my daughter Haley was fourteen, an event rocked her world, and my world had just been rocked by a head-on car accident. It was April 30, 2007. I was rushed to the hospital and was given six pints of blood. I came very close to death before they finally stopped the bleeding. A couple of days later, I went into surgery. I was injured so badly that the doctors doubted I'd ever walk again. If I made it out of surgery, rehab was going to be long and grueling, as many other severely injured people can attest. During that time, Haley started acting out. I didn't know if it was normal teenage experimentation or if she was having trouble coping with my injuries and near-death experience. Whatever the source, she made some bad choices. (By the way, she shared her story in church, and she gave me permission to tell it in the book.)

One night, she went to a friend's house. For some reason, a twenty-one-year-old man was there. When she left to walk home, he offered to walk with her. In an alley, he sexually assaulted her. He told her, "I know your dad is in a wheelchair. If you ever tell anybody what happened tonight, I'll kill him!"

When I found out, I tried to find him, and it wasn't to share the love of Jesus!

Like all sexual assault victims, Haley had trouble processing the violation of her dignity. She tried to cope with her pain and fear by filling her life with danger and excitement. She was caught stealing several times.

During the seven months after the accident, I graduated from a hospital bed to a wheelchair to a walker to a cane. While I had been on leave, the bank eliminated my position due to departmental realignments, but my boss, Cindy Ginn, opened a door for me to apply for another position in Houston. The move didn't improve Haley's decision-making. We took her cell phone away, but she slipped out of the house, asked to borrow someone's phone, and conveniently "forgot" to give it back.

In 2010, we moved to Florida. On her eighteenth birthday, Haley stole a credit card from one of her teachers, bought a ticket to Little Rock, Arkansas, and got on the plane to be with a guy she'd met online.

A few months later, Haley rushed in the door and headed to her bedroom. I could hear a young lady outside in panic. When I opened the door, she was running through our apartment complex yelling, "She stole my wallet! A girl stole my wallet!"

I knew Haley was the one who had stolen the girl's wallet.

I walked quickly to her bedroom. "Why did you do it?" I asked.

"Do what?" She looked defiant.

"Steal that girl's wallet!" I replied.

"I didn't steal anything!" she insisted. "Why don't you believe me? I'm your daughter!"

"Because you did it!"

When I was on a business trip, a Florida State Trooper knocked on our door. Tracy answered it, and the officer asked, "Why did you leave the scene of an accident?"

Surprised, Tracy said, "What? I wasn't in an accident."

The officer described the vehicle, and Tracy told him, "That's my husband's car, and he's out of town."

He barked, "It's been *somewhere*." He held up a license plate. "The car was involved in a hit-and-run accident." Guess who had been driving it . . .

Not long after the incident with the car, Haley was arrested for shoplifting, and Florida doesn't play around with that crime. They put her in the county jail, where Casey Anthony, the mom convicted of killing her toddler daughter, was also incarcerated. Haley was sentenced to ninety days, even though the costume jewelry she'd stolen was worth only about eighteen dollars. Tracy and I visited her, but I refused to pay for bail to get her out. I knew I'd only be throwing money down the drain because she'd skip the court date.

Tracy and I went to see her every day when they offered visitation. The jail had visitors and inmates connect on video screens. Tracy always sat in the chair first, which was directly in front of the other chair, and when our time was half over, we would switch. Haley didn't want to talk to me. She was angry because I wouldn't pay the money to get her out. Time after time, I told her. "No, Haley, I'm not getting you out. I don't trust you, but I love you. This is best for you and for us."

Tracy and I weren't on the same page. She wanted me to pay the bail to get Haley out of jail, but I refused. I'm not sure who was angrier with me, Tracy or Haley. Tracy pleaded with me. We had plenty of money, but money wasn't the issue. I sensed the Lord wanted Haley to stew in jail to get her attention. If I bailed her out, she wouldn't learn a thing.

After about two months, Tracy and I went to see Haley again. Tracy started to sit in front of the screen, but Haley said, "I want to talk to Dad first."

I was more than a little surprised. When I sat down, she looked at me and said, "Listen. Listen. I'm not going to ask you to get me out. I want you to hear what happened." She started crying.

She told me that since the first day in jail, the other women told her, "This is where you belong. You're one of us." That had shaken her to the core.

A local church led by Pastor Clint Brown sponsored chapel services at the jail. My family members, David and Nicole, were guest worship leaders from time to time. When one of the ladies from the church met Haley and asked for her name, the lady asked, "Your name's Binion? What are you doing here? Are you related to David and Nicole?"

Haley nodded. "Yes, we're family. David's dad is my dad's uncle."

She told Haley, "You don't belong here. You have a heritage of ministry." She invited Haley to come to the chapel services, and she did.

The people leading the services led in some songs, and one of the guards heard Haley's beautiful voice. (Hold on. This is where we see the hand of God!)

Haley told me, "Dad, the other day, a fight broke out in one of the pods. The guards struggled to separate the women. One of them ran to our pod and asked me to come with her.

She took me into the pod where the women were fighting and shut the door. Then she told me, 'Sing!'"

"I asked, 'What?'"

"She said, 'Sing!'"

"I started singing, 'I've come to pour my praise on Him like oil from Mary's alabaster box...'"

Haley was really crying now. "Daddy, the power of that worship changed things. The women quit fighting and just listened. I kept singing. I don't know what happened, but I know I'm not supposed to be here. This isn't my future. Daddy, you don't have to get me out. Whatever just happened, that's my future."

A few weeks later, Haley walked out of the county prison with a radically different vision of God and her life. Tracy and I have watched her grow in her faith, and we're equally amazed and thrilled that she said, "Yes!!!" to God during a chaotic fight in a women's pod in a county jail.

Soon, I was transferred back to Texas, and Haley started reconstructing her life around God. We had started Encounter Church, but I was still working at the bank. She sang more often and sometimes participated with the praise team. Then, she became a regular on the team. Her voice was beautiful, but her posture was unlike anyone else. The rest of them were like the "air dancers" at car dealerships—constant, rhythmic, dramatic movement—but Haley's movements were, shall we say, understated.

When our worship pastor left, the Holy Spirit told me to appoint Haley to the role. I instantly reacted, "No! That's a terrible idea. Haven't You heard of nepotism? And besides, it's a conflict of interest."

The Spirit said, "It's My interest. Do it."

I still wasn't buying it. "Lord, pick somebody else . . . anybody else! You used a donkey to speak Your word. Surely you can find somebody else."

My reasoning didn't convince the Lord. He said, "Do what I told you to do."

I met with the worship team and announced that Haley would be taking over. It was a shock to everybody, especially Haley. After the meeting, I told her, "Hon, you dance around the house. Couldn't you move just a little while you're singing at church? This is Encounter Church. It isn't The Church of the Frozen."

Haley is now the lead worship pastor at the Fate campus and the administrative worship pastor over all three campuses. On Sunday mornings, when I see her on stage pointing people to the wonder of God's grace and the power of His glory, I think back to those long, dark years when Tracy and I wondered if the mess she was making of her life would ever change. Her "Yes!" changed everything.

Haley enrolled in The Dwell School of Ministry, which was held at the church where my cousin David and his wife Nicole are pastors. Today, she has a hunger for God's presence. She stays up late to ensure she has her quiet time to read her Bible and pray, and God is doing amazing things to undo the old habits and implant new ones. I told Tracy, "Sometimes, I don't even know who Haley is . . . but I like this one a lot better than the old one! The old one had a hardcore sin nature—probably from your side of the family."

> **WE DON'T HOLD GOD IN OUR HANDS; HE HOLDS US IN HIS.**

She pushed back, "Well, your side isn't perfect!"

"Well, we're a lot closer than your people. Our side is all about souls and slots. (Our family used to own casinos.) But your family is Cuckoo McGoo!"

She didn't think it was as funny as I did.

There's one more part of the story that shows the goodness of God. Before Haley got out of jail, she appeared before the judge. She'd had several drug tests, and they were all clean. To the surprise of all of us, the judge assigned her to the drug program so she would qualify for deferred adjudication, and the conviction wouldn't appear on her record. Thank You, Lord!

The First "Yes!!!"

We naturally focus our attention on *our* decision to follow God with all our hearts, but we need to remember that *His* "Yes!" came first. Our "Yes!" wouldn't and couldn't happen if He hadn't taken the initiative. God created the heavens and the earth, He promised a Redeemer when the first couple turned their backs on Him, He gave instructions to Noah to save a remnant and start over, He appeared to Abram and promised to bless all nations through an heir, He orchestrated events in Joseph's life to save two nations from famine, He chose a shepherd boy to be king of Israel when his own parents didn't even acknowledge that he was their son, and of course, He, in the person of Jesus, stepped out of heaven to live and die for people Paul describes as "enemies of God"—you and me. We don't hold God in our hands; He holds us in His. In his classic book, *Mere Christianity*, C. S. Lewis wrote:

> When you come to knowing God, the initiative lies on His side. If He does not show Himself, nothing you can do will enable you to find Him. And, in fact,

> *He shows much more of Himself to some people than to others—not because He has favourites, but because it is impossible for Him to show Himself to a man whose whole mind and character are in the wrong condition. Just as sunlight, though it has no favourites, cannot be reflected in a dusty mirror as clearly as in a clean one.* [5]

God is assertive with us. He initiates connections, He makes promises, and He establishes covenants. Some have estimated there are more than 8,000 promises in the Scriptures! We don't have quite enough room for all of them (!), but let me highlight a few that are particularly meaningful to me:

> *You will keep in perfect peace those whose minds are steadfast, because they trust in you. Trust in the LORD forever, for the LORD, the LORD himself, is the Rock eternal.*
> **—Isaiah 26:3-4 (NIV)**

> *"For I know the plans I have for you," declares the LORD, "plans to prosper you and not to harm you, plans to give you hope and a future."* **—Jeremiah 29:11 (NIV)**

> *"I will instruct you and teach you in the way you should go; I will counsel you with my loving eye on you."* **—Psalm 32:8 (NIV)**

---

[5] C. S. Lewis, *Mere Christianity* (San Francisco, CA: Harper San Francisco, 1952, 2001), 14.

"Come to me, all you who are weary and burdened, and I will give you rest. Take my yoke upon you and learn from me, for I am gentle and humble in heart, and you will find rest for your souls." **—Matthew 11:28-29 (NIV)**

But he said to me, "My grace is sufficient for you, for my power is made perfect in weakness." Therefore I will boast all the more gladly about my weaknesses, so that Christ's power may rest on me. That is why, for Christ's sake, I delight in weaknesses, in insults, in hardships, in persecutions, in difficulties. For when I am weak, then I am strong.
—2 Corinthians 12:9-10 (NIV)

"Do not be anxious about anything, but in every situation, by prayer and petition, with thanksgiving, present your requests to God. And the peace of God, which transcends all understanding, will guard your hearts and your minds in Christ Jesus." **—Philippians 4:6-7 (NIV)**

"He himself bore our sins" in his body on the cross, so that we might die to sins and live for righteousness; "by his wounds you have been healed." **—1 Peter 2:24 (NIV)**

And we know that in all things God works for the good of those who love him, who have been called according to his purpose. **—Romans 8:28 (NIV)**

When we let the Word "richly dwell" within us, the Spirit whispers affirmations that we belong to God, points out sin so we can repent and experience cleansing, directs us where He wants to use us, and empowers us to be effective. You can't beat that!

TRANSFORMED

Let's return for a moment to Paul's second letter to the Corinthians. We've seen that his "Yes!" to God came in the middle of intense suffering and mistreatment by believers, but Paul was relentlessly faith-filled. Later in the letter, he says that in spite of everything, his "aim," his ambition, is to "be well pleasing" to Jesus (2 Corinthians 5:9). What's our motivation? To impress people with our holiness? To gain power over others? No, it's very different: "For the love of Christ compels us, because we judge thus: that if One died for all, then all died; and He died for all, that those who live should live no longer for themselves, but for Him who died for them and rose again" (vv. 14-15).

God didn't just wallpaper the gospel of grace on our moldy, dilapidated selves. He created something new: "Therefore, if anyone *is* in Christ, *he is* a new creation; old things have passed away; behold, all things have become new" (2 Corinthians 5:17). What's new? Our bodies are the same, our families are the same, but our hearts, perspectives, and desires are radically realigned. Amazingly, He anoints us as His representatives: "Now then, we are ambassadors for Christ, as though God were pleading through us: we implore *you* on Christ's behalf, be reconciled to God" (2 Corinthians 5:20). God has made us junior partners in the family business of redeeming the lost, caring for the least, and doing our part to create God's kingdom on earth as it is in heaven.

What does it look like when the "old things" are replaced by the "new"? Among many transformations, we can expect:

> 1. It changes our connection with God.

We realize *who* we are as people redeemed by the blood of Jesus, and we realize *whose* we are because we belong to our loving Father. Many of us begin this journey with flawed perceptions of God. We saw Him as harsh and demanding, or we believed He was distant and uncaring. He is none of those things. Through Isaiah, God said that He loves us so much that He has our names tattooed on His hands (See Isaiah 49:15-16). (Okay, it says "engraved," not "tattooed," but you get the picture.)

> 2. It changes our view of sin.

Gradually, the things of the world that used to capture our attention begin to fade in importance. Sin is less and less attractive as Jesus becomes more beautiful in our sight. Author and pastor Dane Ortlund explains:

> But we don't kill sin the way a soldier kills an enemy in battle by zeroing in on the enemy himself. Killing sin is a strange battle because it happens by looking away from the sin. By "looking away," I don't mean emptying our minds and trying to create a mental vacuum. I mean, looking at Jesus Christ. In the same way that playing matchbox cars on the front lawn loses its attractiveness when we're invited to spend the afternoon at a NASCAR race, sin loses its appeal as we allow ourselves to be re-enchanted time and again with the unsurpassable beauty of Jesus. . . . Sin feels like riches, but it is counterfeit riches, and one very quickly hits bottom on its pleasures. It doesn't deliver. Christ, on the other hand, is real riches, and one never hits bottom on them. They are unsearchable.[6]

In our response to the Spirit convicting us of sin, many of us go into a ditch on one side or the other. Some of us feel deeply ashamed and think, *I'm such a terrible person! God can't love somebody as awful as me.* We may sing and read about grace, but we don't believe God's grace extends to us. To overcome the horrible shame, we try to feel bad enough long enough to pay for it ourselves. Others are in the other ditch. They deny, minimize, excuse, rationalize, and use other methods to avoid being honest about the sin. And some of us, the really creative ones, vacillate between the two! There's a better way.

---

6 Dane C. Ortlund, *Deeper: Real Change for Real Sinners* (Wheaton, IL: Crossway, 2021), 139.

In his first letter, John wrote:

> If we claim to be without sin [Looking at you, second kind of people], we deceive ourselves and the truth is not in us. If we confess our sins, he is faithful and just and will forgive us our sins and purify us from all unrighteousness [And looking at you, everybody].
> **—1 John 1:8-9 (NIV, author addition)**

Jesus is thrilled to forgive us when we sin. Why? Because He's *already* forgiven us, and He wants us to experience the wonder of His love and forgiveness! Believe it. It's true.

Many of us believe that when we sin, we're like the child who fears his father and says, "I messed up. My dad is going to kill me!" But if we understand and experience God's heart, when we sin, we'll say, "I messed up. I need to tell Dad all about it."

3. It changes our attitude.

I've found that my attitude fluctuates depending on whether my expectations are met. That's not exactly a revolutionary truth. I need to remember that what I deserved was hell and isolation from God, where the worm does not die and the fire isn't quenched, but God has given me an overabundance of pardon, purpose, and power. When I recognize the contrast between what I deserved apart from Christ and what God has given me in Christ, it's not hard to be grateful!

4. It changes our priorities.

We have a yardstick to measure what matters most to us—it's where we spend our time, money, and thoughts. Human nature values the externals, so many people devote tremendous resources to win the game of comparison and competition. But God's priorities are very different. God spoke through Jeremiah to show the contrast:

> *This is what the LORD says:*
> *"Let not the wise boast of their wisdom*
> *or the strong boast of their strength or*
> *the rich boast of their riches,*
> *but let the one who boasts boast about this:that*
> *they have the understanding to know me,*
> *that I am the LORD, who exercises kindness,justice*
> *and righteousness on earth,for in these I delight,"*
> *declares the LORD.*
> **—Jeremiah 9:23-24 (NIV)**

What values do we see in commercials, television shows, and movies? Most often, it's people trying to one-up others in intelligence, power, and wealth. God says, "That's not wise!" A boast is what's most important to us, and God says what's most important is knowing Him and treasuring His kindness, justice, and righteousness above the externals. Our "Yes!" puts God's priorities on the front burner. We want to know and follow His plan. What He directs us to do is the most important thing we can accomplish, even if it makes no sense to anyone else.

5. It changes our relationships.

At one point, when Haley was going off the rails, she called the house. Tracy answered the phone, and Haley asked us to pick her up. Tracy asked, "Where are you?"

She said, "At the strip club."

Both of us were stunned. Tracy told me, "I'm going to get her."

I insisted, "You're not going without me."

She was adamant: "Well, you sure aren't going to a strip club!"

"I didn't say I was going in. We'll find somebody to tell her we're there."

Tracy and I drove to the strip club, and soon, Haley walked out and got in the car. We didn't need to ask for an explanation. She knew she needed a good one! She said, "I was with a friend . . ."

I didn't let her finish. I launched in: "You need the kind of friends who will unthatch a roof and lower you to Jesus, not unthatch their clothes to get money from guys gawking at them and saying, 'Oh, Jesus!'"

We become like the people we spend time with. That's a fact of life. When we first commit to following Jesus, some of us have to take a long, hard look at our "top five" friends. We share the good news of Jesus with them, and hopefully, some of them will say, "Yes!" to Him. But we may realize some of our friends don't exactly point us to righteous living! Solomon taught us, "He who walks with wise *men* will be wise, but the companion of fools will be destroyed" (Proverbs 13:20). It doesn't mean those relationships will end badly, but they become less of a priority as you focus your attention on God's people and God's purposes.

God puts people in our lives to mentor us, equip us, and encourage us to take the next steps on our journey of obedience and blessing. We need to sit at the table of men and women who love God and want every moment of their lives to honor Him. We're in the battle, with these people at our side. We can then say with David, "

You prepare a table before me in the presence of my enemies;

You anoint my head with oil;

My cup runs over (Psalm 23:5).

6. It changes our habits.

Some of us need to change our relationship with food or time or work or television or social media—I could go on, but you understand. When our hearts become more in tune with God's heart, we realize we've wasted too much time on frivolous things, and we make the necessary adjustments. Paul reminded the Ephesians: "Be very careful, then, how you live—not as unwise but as wise, making the most of every opportunity, because the days are evil. Therefore do not be foolish, but understand what the Lord's will is" (Ephesians 5:15-17, NIV). As our leader and guide, Paul gives us a different set of habits to ingrain in our lives:

> *Do not get drunk on wine, which leads to debauchery. Instead, be filled with the Spirit, speaking to one another with psalms, hymns, and songs from the Spirit. Sing and make music from your heart to the Lord, always giving thanks to God the Father for everything, in the name of our Lord Jesus Christ.*
> **—Ephesians 5:15-20 (NIV)**

Habits change when we have the courage to say "No!" to distractions so we can say, "Yes!" to God's best.

> 7. It changes how we invest our time and money.

When we see Jesus as our crucified and risen King, we recognize that He is the sovereign Lord of all, and everything in our hands belongs to Him, including our time and our money. Time is precious. We can waste it, use it in self-destructive ways, or invest it in nurturing our families and spreading the kingdom. In the same way, God entrusts us with resources. When we grasp the fact that all of it is His and our role is to be faithful stewards, our choices to spend, save, and give change. We give out of hearts overflowing with gratitude for all God has given to us, and giving becomes a joyful, self-reinforcing habit.

CHANGING CLOTHES

In his letter to the Ephesians, Paul used the metaphor of changing clothes to illustrate the choices we make to follow Jesus. He instructs us to "put off your old self, which is being corrupted by its deceitful desires." He's talking about our sin nature. When we put it off, we "put on the new self, created to be like God in true righteousness and holiness" (Ephesians 4:22, 24, NIV).

He then gives several case studies to illustrate his point:

- Put off speaking lies and put on speaking truthfully.
- Put off sinful anger that is self-centered and put on godly anger against injustice.
- Put off stealing and put on hard work and generosity.
- Put off unwholesome talk and put on words of encouragement that benefit others.
- Put off bitterness, rage, unrighteous anger, and slander, and put on kindness, compassion, and forgiveness.

Yes, old habits die hard, but we have a power source that can soften the hardest heart. After giving this list of choices, Paul takes us back to the heart of God: "Follow God's example, therefore, as dearly loved children and walk in the way of love, just as Christ loved us and gave himself up for us as a fragrant offering and sacrifice to God" (Ephesians 5:1-2, NIV).

> **TAKE HIS HAND. YOUR "YES!!!" CHANGES EVERYTHING.**

God isn't asking us to do anything He hasn't already done. He speaks truthfully, He's angry when we're victims of injustice, He's incredibly generous to us, He uses the affirmations and promises of Scripture to build us up, and He is infinitely kind, compassionate, and forgiving toward us.

Take His hand. Your "Yes!" changes everything.

THINK ABOUT IT

CHAPTER 2

! Read Ephesians 4:22 and 24. Explain Paul's metaphor of changing clothes. Why is this an important concept in spiritual transformation?

! What's an amazing turnaround story of someone you know who seemed beyond hope? What was the turning point for that person?

! What are two or three promises that mean the most to you? How has God used them in the past? How do you hope He'll use them in the future?

! What difference does it make to see yourself as "a junior partner in the family business" of redeeming the lost, caring for the least, and doing our part to create God's kingdom on earth as it is in heaven?

! Look at the list of transformations. What is one choice you want to (or need to) make in each one?

CONNECTION WITH GOD	
Put off	
Put on	
VIEW OF SIN	
Put off	
Put on	

ATTITUDE	
Put off	
Put on	
PRIORITIES	
Put off	
Put on	
RELATIONSHIPS	
Put off	
Put on	
HABITS	
Put off	
Put on	
TIME AND MONEY	
Put off	
Put on	

> **!** Which of these are you doing pretty well? Which need some attention? What are you going to do about it?

CHAPTER THREE

THE JOURNEY OF SURPRISES

Now to Him who is able to do exceedingly abundantly above all that we ask or think, according to the power that works in us, to Him be glory in the church by Christ Jesus to all generations, forever and ever. Amen.
—Ephesians 3:20-21

I love to read passages in the Bible where God made the unbelievable into reality, but I'm even more thrilled when I get to see God's surprises "up close and in person." Let me share a few stories.

TIM AND COREY

Tim and his wife Corey came to our church from California, where he had been a professional lacrosse player. When I preached a series about the power of every believer's story, I asked Tim to come on stage and tell his. He had been an atheist—as far from God as anyone could be, but Corey was diagnosed with cancer: malignant melanoma, stage 3c. The outlook wasn't good at all. She had just had their first child, a son, but the doctors told her she wasn't going to live to see him grow up. It was a devastating prognosis.

Corey was scared, but she believed God was going to heal her. She asked Him to give her confirmation, and three people, including a letter from a student at the Bethel School of Ministry, told her that God would do the seemingly impossible. Tim envisioned becoming a single dad in the near future, but he watched Corey's faith defy the doctor's prediction. After four months, she had a follow-up appointment with the doctor. He ran tests, but they didn't show that the cancer had spread. In fact, the tests showed that the cancer was gone!

When Tim shared this story sitting on a stool at our church, he had tears in his eyes. He said, "After this, how could I not believe?"

Today, Tim and Corey are both walking with the Lord, growing stronger in their faith every day, with three beautiful children.

CHAIRS
For fifteen months, our church met at an elementary school in Rockwall, Texas, but we needed to find a less expensive facility. We weren't growing fast enough for the giving to

cover the cost. A church offered us space in a strip center they leased, but it was empty. If we rented it, we'd need to upgrade the bathrooms and do more renovations to the meeting room. The school had chairs, but this place didn't. We'd save money on rent, but we'd have to beg, buy, or steal chairs from somewhere. (No, we weren't going to steal, but I wasn't above begging!) It would hold no more than one hundred chairs, and it would be so crowded that we'd have to pass out mouthwash and deodorant in every service.

Randolph, who had been a pastor, and his wife Felicia began attending our church. One day, when we were still meeting in the school and refurbishing the meeting room, he approached me and asked, "Pastor, do you need any chairs?"

I just about fainted, but I was conscious enough to tell him, "Yes! We sure do." I had no idea if he was talking about a dinette set, pews, two recliners, or chairs we could actually use at the church, but this was the most promising conversation I'd had so far.

Randolph explained, "I've got chairs stacked in a storage facility not far from here. Do you want to meet me there to look at them? It's Compass Self-Storage."

I blurted out, "That's where we keep our trailers and our church in a box!"

He gave me the unit number and said, "I'll meet you there."

When I arrived and got out of my truck, I stood at Randolph's unit and could see our trailers. I'd been driving past the answer to my prayer every Sunday!

Randolph raised the door of the storage unit, and I looked at the chairs. They were brown—the same color we'd painted the walls of our new meeting room. I asked, "How many chairs do you have?"

"About seventy-five."

"Perfect," I exclaimed. "That's all we can comfortably put in the room."

I started crying, and I heard the Lord say, "The chairs have been waiting on you. You haven't needed the provision until now, so I waited for your point of need to provide them."

At that moment, if I'd been playing "Let's Make a Deal"[7] and was offered what was behind Door Number 2, I would have said, "No way! God has provided exactly what we need behind Door Number 1!"

THE PRODIGAL RETURNS

My friend Patrick told me the saga of his relationship with his brother. He said, "We were estranged for over forty

---
[7] *Let's Make a Deal*, Joe Behar et al. (December 30, 1963; New York, NY: NBC), Television.

years." I asked him how that happened, and he shared that his brother is an alcoholic who repeatedly lied and stole from their mother and him. Patrick confronted his brother several times, but all he got back was excuses and contempt. "One time when he stole money, his response was, 'I needed it.' He had no conception of honor or responsibility."

Patrick kept praying for his brother, but they saw each other only at their mother's funeral and at a dinner with some other relatives when Patrick invited him. I asked, "How did that go?"

"Terrible," he explained. "He was snarky during the entire dinner, even to my wife, who has always and only been kind to him. After that night, I came real close to giving up."

Five years later, his brother called, seemingly from out of the blue. He told Patrick, "I have a terminal disease, and I need to make things right." He talked about how badly he had treated Patrick, and he apologized for all of it. No excuses this time.

Patrick told him, "I forgave you long ago. I'm so glad to reconnect with you. Let's see where we go from here."

Patrick sent his brother some links to sermons by a pastor who inspires him, and they've had a lot of great conversations about grace, forgiveness, and eternal life. At this writing, his brother is still alive . . . and still soaking in the love and kindness of God. Patrick told me, "When I tell people this story, they often ask if I'm surprised. It's more than that. I'm stunned! In my wildest dreams, I couldn't picture my brother and me talking openly and joyfully about Jesus!"

MARLON

Not long after we started Encounter Church, a pastor who had planted and led two churches in town called me. I had known Marlon when we both worked at the same bank. Our church was still small and struggling, and I didn't know why he wanted to talk. (Maybe he wanted to put me out of my misery. Who knows?) When we talked, he told me, "Pastor Chris, I'd like to come to Encounter Church to be with you."

I had prayed that God would bring some wise, experienced associate pastor, but I'd been in organizational leadership long enough to know I didn't want just anybody. I needed someone with depth and character. My instant response was, "Okay, you can come. You're the associate pastor."

Marlon was surprised and a bit confused. "No, you don't understand. I just want to serve behind the scenes."

"Like an associate pastor. You can help me with all kinds of things." I thought I needed to speak the obvious. "Brother, we can't pay you a dime."

"No problem. I just want to volunteer."

Marlon is a humble, brilliant man. He taught leadership in the corporate world, and he had experience starting churches. Talk about a gift from heaven! When he came, things started to take off. Today, he teaches leadership at the three campuses and has a profound impact on the growth of our church.

I wasn't surprised that God answered my prayer for help, but I was very surprised that God gave me someone with such skill and heart. He would tell you that he was surprised when I asked him to be our associate pastor in our first conversation. It couldn't have worked out any better.

A HISTORY OF SURPRISES

When God commanded Moses to confront Pharaoh and demand the release of the Jewish slaves, He gave his brother Aaron a staff to carry. When they met Pharaoh, he told them to prove themselves, "Show a miracle for yourselves." Moses told Aaron to throw his staff on the ground, and it became a snake. Pretty impressive, don't you think? But Pharaoh called his wise men, sorcerers, and magicians, and all of them threw their staffs on the ground, and they became snakes, too! At that point, I would have thought, *Good grief! I thought we'd have the only stick-snake in town!* But Aaron's snake swallowed all the other snakes. God had one-upped Pharaoh. It was like, "My daddy can whip your daddy!" It was a dramatic representation of God's power over Pharaoh's dark magic (Exodus 7:8-13).

> **SOMETIMES, GOD SURPRISES US WITH INSTRUCTIONS THAT SEEM TO MAKE NO SENSE—ESPECIALLY IF SOMEONE ELSE OFFERS A MORE REASONABLE PATH.**

Gideon was a reluctant leader. During the period of the judges, after the conquest of the Promised Land, tribes continued to harass and attack God's people. When the Midianites oppressed them, Gideon gathered an army of 32,000 to defend the land and the people, but God said, "Not so fast!" He told Gideon to have the soldiers go to the river to drink and retain only those who put their faces near the water and lapped like dogs. That left him with only 300 men, but God promised to use them to win the battle. By most estimates, the Midianites had more than 100,000 men.

One of the maxims of war is to avoid dividing your forces in front of a superior enemy, but Gideon didn't follow that advice. He divided his little band into three groups, each with trumpets and jars containing torches. They surrounded the Midianite camp at night, and on his signal, they blew the trumpets and broke the jars, shining lights all around them. The Midianites were scared and confused. They could have easily defeated the three little Jewish bands, but they mistakenly thought other Midianites were the enemy, so they attacked their own men! It was a colossal victory . . . one Gideon surely didn't expect when he was left with only a handful of soldiers (Judges 7).

Sometimes, God surprises us with instructions that seem to make no sense—especially if someone else offers a more reasonable path. One of the darkest periods in the history of the Jews was the invasion and conquest of Jerusalem by the Babylonians. More than a century earlier, the Assyrians had devastated the ten northern tribes, and now, the Babylonians stood at the capital's gates. The people assumed God would protect them because they believed foreigners could never defile Solomon's beautiful temple. They were wrong. In the early sixth century BC, Nebuchadnezzar led his army in destroying the city and the temple. Many of the city's inhabitants, including Daniel and his three friends, were taken into captivity and marched east to Babylon.

God's people were heartbroken and confused. Had God abandoned them? Would they ever see their homeland again? Not long after they settled in Babylon, the prophet Hananiah proclaimed that their captivity would only last two years. At that time, they'd be freed, and all the temple utensils would be returned to them. He claimed that the Lord said, "I will break the yoke of the king of Babylon." That was music to their ears . . . but it was a lie. Jeremiah, the true prophet, gave the Lord's sentence on Hananiah:

"Behold, I will cast you from the face of the earth. This year you shall die, because you have taught rebellion against the LORD" (Jeremiah 28:16).

Jeremiah told the exiles that the captivity would last seventy years, not two. I'm sure that news created a lot of heartache because many knew they wouldn't live long enough to return to Jerusalem. But Jeremiah had more instructions from the Lord: Settle in, and become a blessing to the people of Babylon:

> *Build houses and dwell in them; plant gardens and eat their fruit. Take wives and beget sons and daughters; and take wives for your sons and give your daughters to husbands, so that they may bear sons and daughters—that you may be increased there, and not diminished. And seek the peace of the city where I have caused you to be carried away captive, and pray to the LORD for it; for in its peace you will have peace.*
> **—Jeremiah 29:5-7**

Isn't that just like God? He wants us to be a blessing to those who disagree with us, who treat us badly, and even become our enemies! When He told Abraham that his descendants would bless all nations, He didn't restrict the circle to those who look like us, think like us, and vote like us. How do we love them? By adapting God's instructions to the exiles: Get to know others so well that you can explain their values better than they can, spend time with them so they trust you, look for common ground instead of points of contention, seek peace with them, and pray for them, "for in [their] peace you will have peace" (Jeremiah 29:7, author addition).

These instructions must have shocked the exiles. They could grit their teeth and survive if they had to make it only two years, but now God required them to have a complete change of mind and heart. The instructions came with a beautiful promise:

> For I know the thoughts that I think toward you, says the LORD, thoughts of peace and not of evil, to give you a future and a hope. Then you will call upon Me and go and pray to Me, and I will listen to you . . . And you will seek Me and find Me, when you search for Me with all your heart. I will be found by you, says the LORD, and I will bring you back from your captivity; I will gather you from all the nations and from all the places where I have driven you, says the LORD, and I will bring you to the place from which I cause you to be carried away captive.
> —Jeremiah 29:11, 13-14

Someday (though not as soon as they hoped), God would make all things right.

God never planned to limit the scope of His love, grace, and power. The Jews were His "chosen race," but they were chosen to be a "light to the world," taking the Good News of the coming Messiah to every corner of the planet. The temple in Jerusalem was inclusive . . . but only kind of. The court of men was closest to where the priests offered sacrifices. Beyond them was the court of women, and at the farthest reaches of the temple complex was the court of the believing Gentiles, which was separated from the rest by a stone wall. In the early church, one of the biggest (actually, *the* biggest) controversies was whether and how to accept Gentiles into the fellowship of Christian believers. Many Jewish leaders assumed Gentiles would need to convert to Judaism before they could be part of their Messiah's family. (That was the problem Paul addressed in his letter to the Galatians, and it was also the topic in the Jerusalem Council.)

Peter was a devout Jew. He was steeped in the traditions and beliefs, including the dietary restrictions, circumcision, and the superiority of the Jewish race. Then, God turned his assumptions upside down. A Roman officer named Cornelius was a "God-fearing Gentile" who lived on the coast of Israel in Caesarea Maritima. He was generous with his money and was devoted to prayer. One day, God gave him a vision and told him to send some men down the coast to Joppa to find Peter.

As the men were on their way, Peter was on the housetop at noon, praying. He got hungry, but while others were preparing lunch, God gave him a vision. He "saw heaven opened and an object like a great sheet bound at the four corners, descending to him and let down to the earth. In it were all kinds of four-footed animals of the earth, wild beasts, creeping things, and birds of the air. And a voice came to him, 'Rise, Peter; kill and eat.'"

That made absolutely no sense to a kosher man! He responded, "Not so, Lord! For I have never eaten anything common or unclean."

The voice spoke again: "What God has cleansed you must not call common" (Acts 10:11-15). The vision and voice were repeated two more times, and then the sheet vanished into heaven. Peter was understandably puzzled. While he was trying to figure it out, three men came to his door, and the Spirit told him to go with them. They explained that Cornelius had sent them, and the pieces of the puzzle began to fall into place in Peter's mind.

> **THE STORY OF THE BIBLE, AND THE GREATEST STORIES OF OUR LIVES, IS THAT GOD WANTS TO BLESS US MORE THAN WE CAN IMAGINE.**

The next day, the four men walked north along the coast to Caesarea to meet Cornelius. Peter, it seemed, wanted to make sure everyone understood that his presence was completely unexpected. He told Cornelius and the others in the room:

> *You know how unlawful it is for a Jewish man to keep company with or go to one of another nation. But God has shown me that I should not call any man common or unclean. Therefore, I came without objection as soon as I was sent for. I ask, then, for what reason have you sent for me?*
> **—Acts 10:28-29**

Cornelius told Peter about his vision, and Peter was convinced. He must have felt equally thrilled and awkward when he said:

> *In truth I perceive that God shows no partiality. But in every nation whoever fears Him and works righteousness is accepted by Him. The word which God sent to the children of Israel, preaching peace through Jesus Christ—He is Lord of all— that word you know, which was proclaimed throughout all Judea, and began from Galilee after the baptism which John preached: how God anointed Jesus of Nazareth with the Holy Spirit and with power, who went about doing good and healing all who were oppressed by the devil, for God was with Him.*
> **—Acts 10:34-38**

While Peter was speaking, he experienced another shock: the Holy Spirit fell on everyone in the room, and the Gentiles spoke in tongues and praised God! Peter finally connected all the dots: "Can anyone forbid water, that these should not be baptized who have received the Holy Spirit just as we *have?*" Cornelius and the other new believers were baptized and accepted, by grace through faith in Jesus, into the family of God (Acts 10:47-48).

The story of the Bible, and the greatest stories of our lives, is that God wants to bless us more than we can imagine. In one of his prayers in his letter to the Ephesians, Paul seems to shout in wonder and praise: "Now to Him who is able to do exceedingly abundantly above all that we ask or think, according to the power that works in us, to Him be glory in the church by Christ Jesus to all generations, forever and ever. Amen" (Ephesians 3:20-21).

BETTER THAN EXPECTED

In these historical accounts and modern stories of God's power, He shows himself better than anyone expected. Paul wrote to the Philippians, "And my God shall supply all your need according to His riches in glory by Christ Jesus" (Philippians 4:19). But we need the eyes of our hearts opened to see His riches in glory. We're not the only ones who have trouble grasping the glory of Jesus: **Jesus wasn't what the religious leaders expected.**

I can imagine the Palm Sunday when Jesus rode into Jerusalem on a donkey with the crowd yelling, "Hosannah! Hosannah to the King," (Matthew 21:9, author paraphrase) but the Pharisees and Sadducees getting frustrated at the noise outside. They might have leaned out the window and yelled, "Y'all be quiet! We're praying that God would send the Messiah!" But instead of worshipping and following Jesus, they plotted to kill Him.

They expected a Messiah who would do three things: cleanse the temple (check), overthrow the Romans by leading a military resistance (nope), and be crowned as the new David king (yeah, but not like they imagined). They believed the Messiah would ride in on a big stallion, not a donkey. They believed the Messiah would lead a successful rebellion, not die in the place of Barabbas, a rebel trying to overthrow the Romans. They believed the Messiah would give them the front-row seats in the new kingdom, not accuse them of being "whitewashed tombs" and "a brood of vipers." They certainly didn't conceive of a dead Messiah!

Jesus was a surprise to them. He was far different from what they imagined a Messiah would be.

Jesus wasn't who John the Baptist expected. We don't get much of the backstory after John baptized his cousin Jesus in the Jordan. When he saw the Holy Spirit descend on Jesus like a dove and heard the Father's voice say, "This is My beloved Son, in whom I am well pleased" (Matthew 3:17), he must have thought, Oh boy! This is it! Jesus is going to make things happen now! *Let's Go Big, Jesus!*

But when John was arrested for not being politically correct in calling out Herod for marrying his brother's wife, it seems languishing in prison gave him second thoughts. He sent some men to Jesus to ask, "Are You the Coming One, or do we look for another?" (Luke 7:20)

Jesus didn't get angry at John's question. He simply answered in a way that showed what a true Messiah would do: "*The* blind see, *the* lame walk, *the* lepers are cleansed, *the* deaf hear, *the* dead are raised, *the* poor have the gospel preached to them." Then He added, "And blessed is *he* who is not offended because of Me" (Luke 7:22-23).

Jesus reminded those who were listening, including John's messengers, of the prophecy of a messenger who would prepare the way for God's Messiah. John had done what God sent him to do, and Jesus was, in fact, God's Anointed One, the Messiah.

John wasn't surprised by Jesus at the baptism, but He was a disappointment to him later. Jesus addressed John's doubts. He was far better than John feared.

Jesus wasn't who the disciples expected.

I'm not going to bash these guys. They answered the call to follow Jesus, and they went with Him through the good times of miracles and the difficult times of opposition. Let's give them credit for that. But they, too, expected Jesus to march into Jerusalem, announce that He was taking over as the new king, lead a revolt, and establish a new government under His leadership.

Again and again, Jesus told them the religious leaders in Jerusalem would kill Him, but they didn't believe it. They may have assumed He was speaking metaphorically. (He spoke in parables, didn't He?) They didn't want to believe He was going to be persecuted and executed—it didn't fit with their plans. On the night Jesus was betrayed, He had His disciples meet with Him for the Passover dinner. It was a solemn occasion, at least for Jesus, because He knew He was about to take the weight of the world's sins on Himself, and it would be excruciating. Something was very odd about this dinner. At the first Passover and all since then, a lamb was slain and cooked, but for this meal, there was no lamb on the table . . . because the Lamb was seated at the table.

When Jesus gave the cup at dinner, He told them, "This cup *is* the new covenant in My blood, which is shed for you" (Luke 22:20), but they still didn't get it. Instead, they argued about who would be the greatest when Jesus took the throne!

> **GOD'S LOVE, POWER, JUSTICE, KINDNESS, WISDOM, AND ALL THE REST ARE PERFECT AND IMMEASURABLE.**

"I'm going to be Secretary of State!"

"No, you're not. You're going to be the Chief Dogcatcher!"

"Oh yeah, well, I'm going to . . ."

What do you imagine Jesus was thinking at that moment? It might have been, *And I'm banking on these guys to lead a worldwide movement based on faith and humility?* Jesus set them straight:

> The kings of the Gentiles exercise lordship over them, and those who exercise authority over them are called 'benefactors.' But not so among you; on the contrary, he who is greatest among you, let him be as the younger, and he who governs as he who serves. For who is greater, he who sits at the table, or he who serves? Is it not he who sits at the table? Yet I am among you as the One who serves.
> **—Luke 22:25-27**

A few hours later, when Jesus was arrested, their illusions of prestige and power vanished, and they ran for their lives! (At least most of them did.)

We don't usually put the religious leaders and the disciples in the same boat, but Jesus was a surprise—and a disappointment—to both of them.

Jesus is always far different, far more, and far better than we can imagine. If we're not surprised by Him, we're not paying attention. One New Testament teacher taught on the Lord's prayer (See Matthew 6:9-13), and when he got to "hallowed be Your name," he said that the holiness of God isn't one of the characteristics; it's a description of all of them. They're all "perfect and immeasurable." God's love, power, justice, kindness, wisdom, and all the rest are perfect and immeasurable, which means we'll spend the rest of our lives—and all eternity—marveling at our limitless God.

The religious leaders, John the Baptist, and the disciples thought they had Jesus pegged, but He surprised all of them. A little humility goes a long way to open doors to greater faith. God spoke through Isaiah:

> *"For My thoughts are not your thoughts,*
> *Nor are your ways My ways," says the LORD.*
> *"For as the heavens are higher than the earth,*
> *So are My ways higher than your ways,*

> *And My thoughts than your thoughts."*
> —Isaiah 55:8-9

AND SOMEDAY...

The story of the Bible is in four parts: creation, fall, redemption, and restoration. The creation account is in the first two chapters of Genesis, but it didn't take long for our ancestors to mess things up! God began to put things back on track with His promise to Abram in Genesis 12, and from there to the end of Revelation, we find the multifaceted story of God going to the greatest lengths to redeem mankind from sin, destruction, and death. We often talk about "going to heaven when we die," but that's not our ultimate destination. We think of "going up" to heaven, but at the end of Revelation, we find that *heaven comes down to earth*. Paul said that Jesus is the "first fruit" of the resurrection from the dead, and in the new heavens and new earth, we'll have resurrected bodies. We'll sing, dance, hug, laugh, and serve in a body something like the one Jesus had after His resurrection. It will be a "spiritual body," which seems to be a contradiction in terms, but that's what Jesus had . . . and has. It's both spiritual and physical, as described in 1 Corinthians 15.

The imagery of Revelation gives us hints of what our ultimate destiny will be like, but it will be far better than we can possibly imagine. Professor N. T. Wright has written and spoken extensively about the new heavens and new earth. In a message, he explained:

> The God in whom we believe is the creator of the world, and he will one day put this world to rights. That solid belief is the bedrock of all Christian faith. God is not going to abolish the universe of space, time and matter; he is going to renew it, to restore it, to fill it with new joy and purpose and delight, to take from it all that has corrupted it. "The wilderness and the dry land shall be glad; the desert shall rejoice and blossom, and rejoice with joy and singing; the desert shall become a pool, and the thirsty ground springs of water." The last book of the Bible ends, not with the company of the saved being taken up into heaven, but with the New Jerusalem coming down from heaven to earth, resulting in God's new creation, new heavens and new earth, in which everything that has been true, lovely, and of good report will be vindicated, enhanced, set free from all pain and sorrow. God himself, it says, will wipe away all tears from all eyes.[8]

Ironically, God wants us to think deeply about this destiny to put everything in our lives in perspective, but it will be so wonderful that it will exceed our fondest hopes. In C. S. Lewis's famous sermon preached during a time in World War II when the Allies were losing almost every battle, he points us to the same hope Wright describes. Lewis says

---
8   Dr. N.T. Wright, "The Road to New Creation," *NT Wright Page*, https://ntwrightpage.com/2016/03/30/the-road-to-new-creation/.

five things will be true for us: we'll be with Christ, our bodies and hearts will be transformed to be like Christ, we'll experience the radiant "glory" of enjoying God's loving presence, we'll enjoy the feast of salvation, and we'll have meaningful roles in the Kingdom—"ruling cities judging angels, being pillars of God's temple."[9] The original couple was created to represent God on the physical earth, and when creation is renewed, we'll represent Him, too.

(All this sounds terrific, but will we be like Adam and Eve in the Garden? If we are, I need to go to the gym and get in better shape! Skinny people don't mind as much as chubby people like me. I'll need at least a fig leaf! A real big one . . . actually, several really big ones.)

How would it affect your attitude today if you knew that tomorrow you'd receive an inheritance of $10 million? How would that affect your anxiety and your worries? The fact is that someday (probably not tomorrow, but you never know), you'll receive an inheritance from God that's worth far more than a trillion dollars! It will be stunning, amazing, and thrilling.

Yes, we have some hints about what that day will be like, but it's like looking at the Rocky Mountains through fog. It'll be bigger, better, and more beautiful than our hearts can conceive.

---

9   C.S. Lewis, "The Weight of Glory," Church of St. Mary the Virgin, Oxford, England, June 8, 1942, https://www.doxaweb.com/assets/weight_of_glory.pdf.

THINK ABOUT IT

CHAPTER 3

! Read Ephesians 3:20-21. What is God saying to you through this passage?

! What is a surprise "God moment" you've heard that inspires you?

! What is the biggest surprise in your walk with God?

! What are two or three misguided conceptions of God that people have these days? (And yes, you can list Rickey Bobby as one of them!)

! Describe how God has expanded and clarified your concept of Him since you became a believer. What difference has it made in your attitude, gratitude, and relationships?

! Is the idea of the glory of the new heavens and new earth new to you? How does it (or might it) give you a stronger hope for the future?

CHAPTER FOUR

OBSTACLES ARE OPPORTUNITIES

"You are My servant,
I have chosen you and have not cast you away:
Fear not, for I am with you;
Be not dismayed, for I am your God.
I will strengthen you,
Yes, I will help you,
I will uphold you with My righteous right hand."
—Isaiah 41:9-10

So far in this book, we've looked at a lot of encouraging passages and stories, but make no mistake, the enemy isn't finished with you. He may have punched you in the gut and pummeled your head, but don't assume the worst is over. If you're committed to the habit of saying "Yes!" to God, he'll come after you more fiercely than ever. Tragically, many Christians mistakenly assume their ticket to heaven is also a "get out of suffering card." Look at it this way: When Jesus said, "Follow Me," where was He going? To the right hand of the Father? Yes, that's right, but not before He was misunderstood by His friends, betrayed by one of them, denied by another, mercilessly attacked by leaders who should have fallen at His feet in reverence and awe, hauled before a kangaroo court and falsely accused, condemned to suffer the most excruciating and humiliating execution known at the time, and mocked as He bled and died for those who nailed Him to that cross (and every other person who ever lived and ever will live). That's where He was going, and He told us to follow Him. Is that what you signed up for? I hope so.

We live comfortable lives, with far more wealth and pleasures than any culture in history. Even most of those who live in relative poverty often have flat-screen televisions and cell phones. It's easy for us to focus on the promises for more and overlook the kingdom assignment to devote every moment to listening and obeying the One who bought us with the steepest price ever paid. We need to remember that Jesus told His first disciples, and He's saying the same thing to us:

> *If anyone desires to come after Me, let him deny himself, and take up his cross, and follow Me. For whoever desires to save his life will lose it, but whoever loses his life for My sake will find it. For what profit is it to a man*

if he gains the whole world, and loses his own soul? Or what will a man give in exchange for his soul?"
—Matthew 16:24-26

Are we reading this message? Are we listening? Are we following?

ROARING LIONS

Walking with Jesus and giving up our self-centered agendas for His sake takes courage. Peter told us bluntly, "Be sober, be vigilant; because your adversary the devil walks about like a roaring lion, seeking whom he may devour" (1 Peter 5:8). My guess is that few of those reading this book have much experience roaming the savannahs of Africa and being attacked by lions. But it happened, and it's wise for us to learn some lessons from the tragedy. Between March and December 1898, workers building the Kenya-Uganda Railway were terrorized by two mane-less male lions. Lt. Colonel John Henry Patterson arrived in Tsavo a few days before some workers disappeared from their camp. He assumed it was an isolated instance, but months later, the lions returned. They killed and devoured workers almost every day. Crews tried everything to protect the men, building big fires and making fences from the branches of whistling thorn trees. Nothing worked. The lions leaped over or crawled under the fences, and they weren't afraid of the fires. Patterson called experienced hunters to join him in finding and killing the beasts. The first several hunts weren't successful, but Patterson finally killed one on December 9, and the second took nine rounds from high-powered rifles before it died on December 29. The first lion measured nine feet eight inches. Eight men were required to carry it back to the camp. In all, it was estimated that the lions killed and ate 135 men. In a report on the delay caused by the man-eaters, the British Prime Minister told the House of Lords:

> *The whole of the works were put to a stop because a pair of man-eating lions appeared in the locality and conceived a most unfortunate taste for our workmen. At last the labourers entirely declined to carry on unless they were guarded by iron entrenchments. Of course it is difficult to work a railway under these conditions and until we found an enthusiastic sportsman to get rid of these lions our enterprise was seriously hindered.*[10]

The story was captured in the movie, *The Ghost and the Darkness*.[11] The lions are mounted and can be seen at the Field Museum in Chicago. Our enemy wants to strike fear in us and stop our work for the Lord. Like the lions of Tsavo, he's sneaky and ravenous.

During the Babylonian captivity, Daniel served King Darius. Daniel was a godly man who trusted God even when he was

---
10 J. H. Patterson, *The Man-eaters of Tsavo and Other East African* Adventures (New York, NY: MacMillan and Co., 1908), 104.
11 Stephen Hopkins, *The Ghost and the Darkness* (October 11, 1996; Los Angeles, CA: Paramount Pictures).

far from home and was asked to serve a king other than one in Jerusalem. The king's other advisors were jealous of Daniel, and they conspired to trick the king into issuing a decree forbidding prayer to anyone but himself for thirty days. Punishment for disobedience was being thrown into the lions' den. The advisors knew Daniel was loyal to his God and would keep praying. He would be punished, even though Darius loved him.

To no one's surprise, Daniel continued to pray three times a day, but now in front of a window so everyone could see him. When the advisors reported him, the king looked for a way to avoid the sentence of death. He was:

> ... *greatly displeased with himself, and set his heart on Daniel to deliver him; and he labored till the going down of the sun to deliver him. Then these men approached the king, and said to the king, 'Know, O king, that it is the law of the Medes and Persians that no decree or statute which the king establishes may be changed.*
> **—Daniel 6:14-15**

Darius was forced to follow through with the decree, but he believed Daniel's God would deliver him. He told Daniel, "Your God, whom you serve continually, He will deliver you." Daniel was thrown into the den, and a stone was set over the opening.

The king spent the night fasting and sleepless. Early the next morning, he hurried to the den and cried out, "Daniel, servant of the living God, has your God, whom you serve continually, been able to deliver you from the lions?"

> **TEMPTATION IS USUALLY COUPLED WITH ATTRACTIVE LIES.**

Daniel's voice was clear and strong: "O king, live forever! My God sent His angel and shut the lions' mouths, so that they have not hurt me, because I was found innocent before Him; and also, O king, I have done no wrong before you" (Daniel 6:21-22).

Darius turned the tables on Daniel's accusers. He threw them and their families into the lions' den, and the beasts must have worked up quite an appetite while Daniel was with them!

Our enemy uses three primary, overlapping ploys to harm us: temptation, deception, and accusation. He tempted Eve in the Garden by telling her a deceptive lie that she could "be like God." That's the essence of all temptation: that we can be our own masters and have things the way we want them. Eve (with Adam tagging along) walked past all the other trees with delicious fruit to get to the one tree that would poison her. Temptation is usually coupled with attractive lies. Satan called God's goodness into question, implying that he had a better plan for Eve than God. Satan is "the accuser of [the] brethren" (Revelation 12:10, NIV, author addition). He was behind the lies told by Darius's officials. His goal wasn't just to slow Daniel's impact; it was to get rid of him and shame him as an enemy of the king! How does he accuse us? We hear harsh whispers, "You're no good." "You can't do anything right." "You're worthless, hopeless, and helpless." And many more. But most often, it sounds like it's coming from us, not the devil: "*I'm* no good." "*I* can't do anything right." "*I'm* worthless, hopeless, and helpless." The accusations are designed to crush our spirits, inflame our shame, and cause us to doubt God's grace and love.

Some of us, especially those who experienced traumatic childhoods, often internalize self-condemnation because self-hatred seems perfectly right and normal. We emotionally beat ourselves bloody because we don't think we deserve anything better. We can read about God's great love and sing the great hymns of grace, but they seem to bounce off our hearts. Psychologist Pete Walker coined the term "inner critic" to describe the "voices" in the heads of many of us. He writes:

> The "inner critic" weds shame and self-hate about imperfection to fear of abandonment, and mercilessly drive the psyche with the entwined serpents of perfectionism and endangerment. Recovering

> *individuals must learn to recognize, confront and disidentify from the many inner critic processes that tumble them back in emotional time to the awful feelings of overwhelming fear, self-hate, hopelessness and self-disgust that were part and parcel of their original childhood abandonment.*[12]

Does that description sound familiar? There's hope for you! If it doesn't, thank God that you didn't grow up internalizing toxic, soul-crushing messages.

The enemy still tries to "steal, kill, and destroy," but Jesus points us to a different future: "I have come that they may have life, and that they may have it more abundantly" (John 10:10).

We are inundated by messages from television, movies, and social media. They show gorgeous women and handsome men, and the clear implication is that if you buy their bread, insurance, beer, breakfast cereal, and every other commodity, you'll be as good-looking and popular as they are. It's an obvious lie, isn't it? But then, why do we believe it? The only commercials with large people are the "before" stories of weight loss. We've become obsessed with our figures. I went to the doctor for a check-up. My blood pressure was 120 over 70, my heart rate was 65, and

---

[12] Pete Walker, "Shrinking the Inner Critic in Complex PTSD," *Pete Walker Page,* http://www.petewalker.com/shrinkingInnerCritic.htm.

my cholesterol was 162. The little Filipino doctor told me, "You have one problem."

I asked, "What's that?"

"You're fat."

I leaned back in astonishment. I asked, "What! When did that happen? When I looked in the mirror this morning, I looked skinny." After a few seconds, I asked him, "Are you sure it's not just big bones? All the Binions have big bones."

He shook his head. "No bones that big."

I'm not suggesting we give up watching sports or the news or *The Beverly Hillbillies*,[13] but I'm recommending that we develop the habit of asking two questions when the commercials are on: What is the surface promise of the ad? Clean teeth, tasty food, peace of mind, and so on. But then ask, What's the underlying promise? In many cases, the real promise is that if we use a particular brand of toothpaste, we'll be immensely popular and surrounded by beautiful people, our lives will be easy and pleasant, and we'll be rich beyond our wildest dreams. Yeah, that sounds good, doesn't it? But it's a lie of the enemy. As Peter warned, be alert.

---

13 *The Beverly Hillbillies,* Penelope Spheeris (September 26, 1962-March 23, 1971; Los Angeles, CA: CBS), Television.

THE DEMONIC AMONG US

Sometimes, people ask me if I see demon possession today like they did in the first century. I believe demonic oppression (of believers) and possession (of unbelievers) are on the rise, but it's seldom as evident as throwing a boy into a fire or driving someone to live naked among tombs. Far more often, we make good things into ultimate things, putting success, pleasure, and approval on the throne in our hearts, giving allegiance to them more than to God. That, I believe, is the most common and most powerful strategy of the devil. In a commencement address at Kenyon College, novelist David Foster Wallace warned the graduates:

> *If you worship money and things—if they are where you tap real meaning in life—then you will never have enough. Never feel you have enough. It's the truth. Worship your own body and beauty and sexual allure and you will always feel ugly, and when time and age start showing, you will die a million deaths before they finally plant you. On one level, we all know this stuff already—it's been codified as myths, proverbs, clichés, bromides, epigrams, parables: the skeleton of every great story. The trick is keeping the truth up front in daily consciousness. Worship power—you will feel weak and afraid, and you will need ever more power over others to keep the fear at bay. Worship your intellect, being seen as smart—you will end*

up feeling stupid, a fraud, always on the verge of being found out.¹⁴

If we value anything or anyone other than God as our top priority, we'll be excited at first, but inevitably, we'll end up disappointed, empty, and confused. It's certainly not wrong to be successful, good-looking, smart, popular, and wealthy, but if these are our primary passions, we've made them into idols—not little statues we bow down to, but the things in which we invest too much of our money, time, and hearts. In his first letter, John addressed this problem and gave this warning:

> *Do not love the world or the things in the world. If anyone loves the world, the love of the Father is not in him. For all that is in the world—the lust of the flesh, the lust of the eyes, and the pride of life—is not of the Father but is of the world. And the world is passing away, and the lust of it; but he who does the will of God abides forever.*
> **—1 John 2:15-17**

Satan loves to tempt us with these secondary pursuits; he deceives us that these will give ultimate meaning, and then he accuses us of being terrible, awful Christians when we realize we've mixed up our priorities. He's very active in our day-to-day lives.

---

14 Wallace, David Foster. "This Is Water." Commencement Speech, Kenyon College, filmed June 11, 2019, video of lecture, 21:56, https://www.youtube.com/watch?v=xoblutORPNA.

THE CYCLE OF A DREAM

Great victories happen only when we encounter daunting challenges. We can see "the life cycle of a dream" in the Scriptures, in our favorite novels, and in great movies. The cycle includes birth, death, rebirth, and fulfillment. The birth is the initial vision; the idea that revs your engines and consumes your daydreams. It might be starting a business, inventing a product, launching a ministry, having a child, or anything else that inspires a better future. (Someone asked me if buying a bass boat is this kind of dream. I said, "Yes, and so is selling it!")

> **WE'RE HEARTBROKEN BY THE DEATH, BUT THE CYCLE OF LIFE MAKES DEATH A NECESSITY.**

The dream's death may come slowly or suddenly. In Ernest Hemingway's novel *The Sun Also Rises*, Bill asks Mike, "How did you go bankrupt?" Mike responds, "Gradually, then suddenly."[15] We may hang on to hope for a long time, looking for a turnaround that never comes, or death may happen like the collapse of a poorly-built skyscraper in an earthquake—instantaneous, with only a cloud of dust remaining. Tracy and I watched, prayed, and hoped Haley

---
15 Ernest Hemingway, *The Sun Also Rises* (New York, NY: Scribner, 1926).

would have a revelation and come back to God . . . and to us. It was like watching a crucifixion—a long, slow, painful death of our dream for our daughter. For others, funding for the new business wasn't sufficient, and the new company went under, someone else beat the product we invented in the market, the people we counted on to start the ministry backed out, or we hit a submerged tree in our bass boat.

We're heartbroken by the death, but the cycle of life makes death a necessity. On the other side is something better: our motives may be purified, our ideas might be clearer, and we have more wisdom about the trajectory toward success. Jesus said, "Most assuredly, I say to you, unless a grain of wheat falls into the ground and dies, it remains alone; but if it dies, it produces much grain" (John 12:24). That's our hope when a dream dies.

Rebirth sometimes seems too good to be true. Is there really a better future after all? It can be so fragile and faint that we don't recognize it at first, but gradually, inspiration and creativity revive. Then we can sing like Gordon Lightfoot, "Sometimes a broken dream will make you sad or make you mean. Sometimes things ain't as bad as they seem."[16] When Haley was arrested and put in jail, we wondered if that was the end for her. The other women in her pod told her, "You belong here." Did she? Was this a glimpse into a dark future for our baby girl? It turns out that being

---

16 Gordon Lightfoot, vocalist, "Broken Dreams" by Gordon Lightfoot, released 1983, track 10 on *Salute*, Warner Bros. Records.

in jail provided her with an opportunity to connect with someone who loved her, to be with people who love Jesus, and to use her amazing voice in a way none of us could have predicted. It was the first glimmer of her rebirth.

> **QUITTING IS EASY; PERSEVERING TAKES GUTS.**

Sometimes, the rebirth is just a better version of the original dream, but quite often, it's significantly different. We've learned something from our experience in the first three parts of the cycle, and now we bring insights, caution, experience, creativity, and boldness we didn't have before.

The fulfillment of the new, refined, redirected dream is thrilling. I can't tell you what a delight (and relief) it was to see Haley begin to walk with Jesus, use her voice to inspire others, and relate to Tracy and me with increasing honesty, integrity, and respect. (Even as I write this, I can't decide whether to shout praise to God or cry like a baby over the miracle.)

What does it take to keep going after the death of our dreams? Tenacity. Resilience. Hope. Quitting is easy; persevering takes guts. In the heartache of the loss, it's easy to go down the hole of self-pity and resentment. We feel justified in wallowing in that mud because, we're sure, life isn't fair, God didn't come through for us like He did for someone else, and if we'd had better breaks, we'd be on top of the world. That analysis certainly feels good and right and normal, but if we let it take root in our hearts, it'll crowd out faith, hope, and love—and we'll be stuck, groveling in our complaints until we come to our senses.

A PERFECT OPPORTUNITY

Obstacles are imminent—they're all around us all the time. If we deny they exist, minimize them, or run from them, we'll miss opportunities to shine the light of Christ into the darkness of our world. Do you remember the song, "They'll know we are Christians by our love"?[17] Throughout history, when believers have loved well, amazing things have happened: hospitals were built, orphanages cared for abandoned children, slavery was abolished, unwed mothers found safe havens, workers had better conditions and wages, the homeless were housed, and the hungry fed. Christians inaugurated all of these efforts, and they're still in effect today.

There may be no better example of an obstacle becoming an opportunity than the Christians' response during two plagues in the Roman Empire. The first one, which began about 155 AD and lasted fifteen years, was probably smallpox, and the second, around 250 to 262 AD, may

---
[17] Jars of Clay, vocalists, "They'll Know We Are Christians by Our Love" by Peter Scholtes, released March 22, 2005, track 13 on *Redemption Songs*, F.E.L. Publications.

have been measles. In each one, about a fourth of the entire population of the empire died. (And we thought COVID-19 was bad!) The pagan doctors fled the cities to save their own lives, and many pagans left their family members to die alone. Amazingly, Christians stepped in to care for their own *and* the sick pagans. Dionysius, the bishop of Alexandria, gives us a glimpse of love and sacrifice:

> *Most of our brother Christians showed unbounded love and loyalty, never sparing themselves and thinking only of one another. Heedless of danger, they took charge of the sick, attending to their every need and ministering to them in Christ, and with them departed this life serenely happy; for they were infected by others with the disease, drawing on themselves the sickness of their neighbors and cheerfully accepting their pains. Many, in nursing and curing others, transferred their death to themselves and died in their stead.*

Dionysius drew a clear contrast with the behavior of the pagans:

> *But with the heathen, everything was quite otherwise. They deserted those who began to be sick and fled from their dearest friends. They shunned any participation or fellowship with death, yet,*

with all their precautions, it was not easy for them to escape.[18]

A modern observer, Glen Scrivener wrote:

> The third-century plague found in the church a Spirit-filled people, willing to walk the way of their Master. Plagues intensify the natural course of life. They intensify our own sense of mortality and frailty. They also intensify opportunities to display countercultural, counter-conditional love.
>
> Christian death rates were significantly lower than those of the general population (perhaps only 10 percent, though the word "only" is a fearful qualifier). The mutual love of brothers and sisters in Christ meant that, on the one hand, those who provided care were at a higher risk of infection, but on the other, those who were infected had better survival rates. As these Christians made themselves vulnerable to death, they actually found life. Once the plague had swept through, Christians were stronger. They were stronger as a proportion of society, since more of them survived. They had more resilience because they had a robust hope in the face of death. And they were stronger as communities, forging even closer bonds through the sufferings they'd faced.[19]

---

18 Eusebius, *Eccl. Hist.* 7.22.7–10.
19 Glen Scrivener, "Responding to Pandemics: 4 Lessons from Church History," *Gospel Coalition*, 16 Mar. 2020, https://www.thegospelcoalition.org/article/4-lessons-church-history/.

In 165 AD, the church was only in the largest cities and met only in house churches (no megachurches yet), comprising less than one-tenth of one percent of the population of the Roman Empire, but after the love displayed by believers in the two devastating plagues, the church grew to over half of the empire's population by 350 AD.[20] How did this amazing growth happen? Because ordinary Christians were moved by the sacrifice of Jesus for them and were willing to sacrifice themselves for others—not just their own, but *all* others.

KEEP GOING

Jesus tells us to follow Him, and Paul told the Philippians to follow him as he follows Jesus: "The things which you learned and received and heard and saw in me, these do, and the God of peace will be with you" (Philippians 4:9). What did they learn, receive, hear, and see in Paul? That he relentlessly followed Jesus no matter what it cost him. Through thick and thin, success and opposition, Paul kept going. I mentioned that his second letter to the Corinthians was a defense of his role as an apostle. He defended himself by pointing to the fact that no one would choose to suffer for the faith if he didn't have to! I can imagine him scrolling through his memory of all the hardships he had faced, and then he listed them:

---

20 Rodney Stark, *The Rise of Christianity: How the Obscure, Marginal Jesus Movement Became the Dominant Religious Force in the Western World in a Few Centuries* (San Francisco, CA: HarperSanFrancisco: 1997).

From the Jews five times I received forty stripes minus one. Three times I was beaten with rods; once I was stoned; three times I was shipwrecked; a night and a day I have been in the deep; in journeys often, in perils of waters, in perils of robbers, in perils of my own countrymen, in perils of the Gentiles, in perils in the city, in perils in the wilderness, in perils in the sea, in perils among false brethren; in weariness and toil, in sleeplessness often, in hunger and thirst, in fastings often, in cold and nakedness.

Did Paul become bitter about all this? Did he think he'd gotten a raw deal? No, he continued to pour himself into the lives of those God had put into his care. He continued, "besides the other things, what comes upon me daily: my deep concern for all the churches. Who is weak, and I am not weak? Who is made to stumble, and I do not burn *with indignation?*" (2 Corinthians 11:24-29)

TO PAUL, EVERY OBSTACLE WAS AN OPPORTUNITY.

On his final trip to Jerusalem to take an offering he had collected from the churches in Greece, Paul stopped to meet with the elders from Ephesus. We think of Paul as the ultimate tough guy, and he was, but he was also as tender as a mother. He recounted how he loved them, and he reminded them of his suffering. Then he told them, "But none of these things move me; nor do I count my life dear to myself, so that I may finish my race with joy, and the ministry which I received from the Lord Jesus, to testify to the gospel of the grace of God" (Acts 20:24).

At the end of their meeting, Paul knelt and prayed with the elders. Luke takes us to the scene: "Then they all wept freely, and fell on Paul's neck and kissed him, sorrowing most of all for the words which he spoke, that they would see his face no more. And they accompanied him to the ship" (Acts 20:37-38).

To Paul, every obstacle was an opportunity. Even in prison, he shared his faith and saw people come to Christ. Our obstacles may be opposition from family members or friends who think we've lost our minds because we're committed to Jesus, but it's probably nothing like what Paul suffered. No, our obstacles are more likely to be wayward children, health concerns, relational strains, a demanding boss, and other problems of that nature. These are hard—I'm not suggesting they're easy—but we have a Savior who went to the cross to demonstrate His love for us, and we have examples in the Scriptures, and hopefully, in our circle of friends, who remind us to trust God no matter what happens . . . because obstacles are opportunities.

Remember *who* you are and *whose* you are. God spoke through Isaiah:

> *You are My servant,*
> *I have chosen you and have not cast you away:*
> *Fear not, for I am with you;*
> *Be not dismayed, for I am your God.*
> *I will strengthen you,*
> *Yes, I will help you,*
> *I will uphold you with My righteous right hand.*
> **—Isaiah 41:9-10**

THINK ABOUT IT

CHAPTER 4

! Look again at Isaiah 41:9-10. What are some ways that having a strong foundation of our identity gives us the courage to face adversities?

! What are some ways Satan weaves temptation, deception, and accusation together to crush our spirits and cause us to doubt God's goodness? Give an example or two.

! How would you define and describe "the inner critic"? What are the messages? What do they sound like? What impact do they have?

! Think of two popular commercials on television. What's the surface promise? What's the underlying, real promise? How would it help you to identify these promises as you watch television?

! Read the quote by David Foster Wallace again. Do you think his term "worship" is too strong? Why or why not? Do you agree or disagree with the outcomes of the secondary things he mentions (appearance, intellect, wealth, etc.)?

! Have you experienced the cycle of a dream? How did you respond when it died? How was it resurrected?

! Paul followed Jesus, and the Philippians followed Paul. Who is following you? What impact are you having on them?

CHAPTER FIVE

THE PROMISE IS A PROCESS

I wait for the LORD, my soul waits,
And in His word I do hope.
My soul waits for the Lord
More than those who watch for the morning—
Yes, more than those who watch for the morning.
—Psalm 130:5-6

In 2019, Encounter Church was two years old, and I was ready to quit. I was still working at the bank while I led the church, and I was exhausted. I would have been energized if we had seen God grow the church, but from our opening week of 134, we were down to about thirty. I had two jobs, I was a stand-up comedian, I wrote music, and I was a husband and father. My stress level was at DEFCON 1, and my energy level was at the bottom of the Dead Sea.

I had enjoyed business success, was in demand for my comedy, and had won awards for songs I'd written, but the church wasn't on my list of successes. I try to be objective about everything I do, and my analysis of my leadership at Encounter Church told me I wasn't the man for the job. It wasn't that I hadn't seen success in ministry over the course of my life. Tracy and I had served in youth ministry in several churches and had seen each one grow very large. Some said our youth ministry at Pastor Collins's church in Newport News was one of the largest in the country. I don't know about that, but we had always been in the sweet spot of God's blessing . . . until now.

As Encounter Church continued to struggle, I imagined my kids driving by the building years later and telling their spouse and children, "Yeah, that's where my dad was a pastor. It didn't work out." I didn't want them to see me as a failure, and I didn't want them to see God as unfaithful. These fears consumed much of my waking hours, either clear and crisp in my thinking or as sinister background music.

One day during some of my darkest moments, I heard a voice in my head that said, "God said to plant the church, but did He tell you to be the pastor?" It was just like Satan's deception in the Garden, and just like Eve, I thought it made perfect sense.

I started making plans. I met with my friend Bryan, who pastors a church near ours, and said, "Hey, I've got an idea. Why don't you take over our church and make it one of your church's campuses?"

I could sense the wheels turning in his mind, and finally, he said, "If we take it, we'll close it down for six months and reopen it with our leaders and our culture."

I felt like his words had stabbed me in the heart. I pushed back, "I don't want those thirty people to be homeless for six months." Then I had an idea. "Look, I make plenty of money at the bank. Tracy and I will pay the bills while the church is in transition to become your campus. You can replace our leaders with ones you pick. That's how business mergers happen. We can do that here." I let that sink in, and then I continued, "Obviously, one of the people you'll replace is me. I'll come to your campus, and you can install a new campus pastor at Encounter. I'll do everything I can to make the transition a success."

Bryan told me, "We would have to close it."

Although he wouldn't budge, I was still getting excited about my plan. I believed God had given me a solution to our church's struggles and my disappointment, and I was eager to put the plan in motion, if I could just persuade Bryan... oh, and then Tracy. When I got home, I enthusiastically laid out the plan and told her how I thought the Lord had given it to me. She let me utter the last syllable of my brilliant strategy before she said emphatically, "No way! We're not doing that. Not now. Not ever!"

I was just a touch defensive. "How do you know?"

She didn't miss a beat. "Because that's not what God called you to do. He called you to be the pastor of this church."

It wasn't a redo of The Exorcist,[21] but I asked, "Did He?"

Tracy looked shocked. I continued, "The Lord told us to plant the church, but He didn't say we need to pastor it. Don't you remember? I never wanted to be a pastor."

She was done with me for the moment. "We'll talk later."

Sometime after that conversation, she spent time in prayer. She told God, "Lord, Chris isn't a quitter. I've never seen him quit at anything. Help me figure this out so I can help him recommit to be the pastor of the church."

The Lord spoke to her. She came out of her prayer time and told me, "The Lord said to give it one more year."

I couldn't argue with that, but I wasn't willing to make the commitment just yet. After two weeks of prayer, I told her,

---

21 William Friedkin, *The Exorcist* (Decembre 26, 1973; Burbank, CA: Warner Bros.).

"Okay, I'll give it a year, but I fully intend to go back to my plan with Brian at that point."

She realized I was at least partially willing, so she said, "Okay, we'll talk about it then."

The waiting started that day. A week or two later, our worship leader left the church, and her husband had done the AV to put the words of songs on the screen. In one stroke, we lost two key people. I asked Haley to take over, but she was reluctant. I wasn't exactly a man of great faith. I prayed, "Lord, I told you I'd give it a year, but this isn't a good start on a turnaround!"

Again and again, I sensed God say, "Just say, 'Yes!' each time I ask you to do something. You said, 'Yes!' to a year. Now keep going."

> **I HADN'T HEARD FROM GOD, BUT IT DIDN'T BOTHER ME BECAUSE I WAS DOING WHAT HE TOLD ME TO DO.**

We were in the middle of twenty-one days of prayer and fasting, but I sensed the Lord wanted me to go for forty days. Fasting is a lost practice for many Christians today. Sometimes people tell me things like, "I'm going to fast from jogging." I ask, "Do you jog now?" The answer is, "No, but I'm not going to start during the fast." Others say, "I'm fasting from social media," but they're only fasting from Snapchat, not Facebook, X, or Instagram. I have to remind myself, "Judge not, Chris."

Since God had directed me to fast almost twice as long as the rest of the church, I thought this would be the most amazing, intimate time with Him I'd ever had. Wrong. The heavens were covered with iron plates. I heard no word, felt no presence, and sensed no direction, but I knew God wanted me to be obedient to the last thing He told me to do, which was to fast and pray for forty days.

I started having some physical problems, including pretty intense pain in my kidneys. I went to a doctor who examined me. When I told her I'd been fasting, she said, "You're too big (she meant fat) to fast this long. Your body is starting to shut down. Have you ever fasted this long before?"

I pointed to my belly and asked, "Does it look like I fast a lot?"

She laughed and told me, "You need to talk to God again and ask Him if you got the forty days right."

Tracy, who decided to join me on the fast, and I started eating one meal a day, but you couldn't call it a meal. It fit in a bottle cap. If I had one chicken nugget, I felt like I'd had four helpings of everything at Thanksgiving and needed to put on sweatpants.

I hadn't heard from God, but it didn't bother me because I was doing what He told me to do. I was all set for an outpouring of His blessings on me, our family, and especially the church. Then we heard about a strange virus that originated in China. Over the next few months, COVID-19 closed businesses and churches, and more than a million people died. Fear was coupled with anger over mask mandates and school closings. When the scope of the lockdowns became evident, I told Tracy, "We should have given the church away when we still had people who attended."

For almost two months, I heard nothing from God, and then He spoke, "Go back to church."

There was a little problem, though. The government wasn't allowing churches to open. I remembered what Samuel told King Saul when he didn't follow the Lord's command: "For rebellion *is as* the sin of witchcraft, And stubbornness *is as* iniquity and idolatry" (1 Samuel 15:23). I had a choice: to obey God or obey the government. I picked God.

A few days later, Texas Governor Abbott announced that churches could open again, but only at twenty-five percent capacity. We were well under that number with our seating capacity.

Studies show that some who left the church during the pandemic never returned. That wasn't true for Encounter Church. When we opened, the thirty people showed up, and in a couple of weeks, fifty-two new people came . . . and over half of them came back. We grew from thirty to almost seventy in a few weeks!

Almost one year to the day after Tracy and I committed to give God one more year, the congregation had grown to over one hundred and twenty. Four hundred percent! We also moved across the parking lot to a standalone church facility right on the freeway. God had done more than I had believed He would.

Waiting on God was one of the hardest things I've ever done. During much of that time, God was silent, and I had to keep going based on what He'd told me in the past. God may have been quiet, but the enemy wasn't! Doubts, accusations, and fears were a daily occurrence, but I chose to say, "Yes!!!" anyway . . . and on the days I wasn't sure I made the right choice, Tracy was right there to remind me.

A friend asked me, "What's the most valuable lesson you learned from waiting?"

I answered, "Stay the course when you don't hear His voice." I added, "What was the last thing you heard from God? Keep doing that until He speaks again. You'll never get the *next* unless you're faithful in the *now*."

WATCHMEN

The Psalms contain a set of songs that pilgrims sang on their walk over to Jerusalem to participate in a feast. They're called the "Songs of Ascents." One of these gives us a picture of what it means to wait for the Lord:

> *I wait for the LORD, my soul waits,*
> *And in His word I do hope.*
> *My soul waits for the Lord*
> *More than those who watch for the morning—*
> *Yes, more than those who watch for the morning.*
> **—Psalm 130:5-6**

God's "word" is both the written Word and the incarnate Word. One tells us of God's promises, the other of His infinite love and grace. When we're forced to wait for God's answers, we need to lean hard into both. We study the Bible to see the patterns of how God worked in and through His people during prolonged, difficult times.

- Abraham and Sarah had to wait twenty-five years for God to fulfill His promise.
- Moses lived in Midian for forty years before God gave him a new mission.
- God led His people to the banks of the Jordan, but when Joshua led them across, it took years of bloody fighting to secure the land for the Jews. It wasn't a Disney cruise!

- David was anointed king but had to wait fifteen years until Saul was killed in battle, and then he was crowned king of Judah ("praise") before he became king of Israel ("the people").
- Elijah waited three and a half years for rain to break the devastating drought.
- God's people waited in exile in Babylon for seventy years.
- The disciples had to wait in Jerusalem for the promised Holy Spirit to come.

These examples (and many more) show us that waiting is "standard operating procedure" for people who follow God.

A second point in the Song of Ascents is that we need to wait expectantly. Waiting on God isn't just passing time. It's clinging to the hope that God will come through, maybe like we envisioned, but probably in a way that's different from our expectations. The psalmist said that he waited "more than those who watch for the morning." This is the image of guards in the watchtowers around the city. During the night, enemy soldiers could creep toward the city, but the first light of dawn would reveal any danger. All night, the guards wondered what was going on out there in the darkness. Their hope was in the certainty of the sun rising in the east. That's the certainty we have of God showing up—in His way and in His timing to accomplish His purposes.

A NEW THING

We live in the overlap of eons. The ancient Jews expected the old eon to end when the Messiah came to establish His kingdom, but God had other plans. The old eon of sin, death, and struggle continues even when the Messiah came and inaugurated His kingdom. We live in both the *already* and the *not yet*—many of the promises of God have already been fulfilled: we have forgiveness, adoption, purpose, and the presence of God now. But some of the promises have yet to be fulfilled: we wait for the eradication of sin and sorrow, the resurrection of our bodies, and our ultimate destination of the new heavens and new earth.

Through Jesus, God has transformed our condition, identity, and future. We were lost, but we're found; we were enemies of God, but now we're sons and daughters; we had no hope, but now we live in the loving presence of God with the certainty of life everlasting. Isaiah quotes God's promise that is fulfilled in Jesus:

> *Behold, I will do a new thing,*
> *Now it shall spring forth;*
> *Shall you not know it?*
> *I will even make a road in the wilderness*
> *And rivers in the desert.*
> —Isaiah 43:19

For us, the "new thing" begins the instant we trust in Christ and are "rescued from the dominion of darkness and brought us into the kingdom of the Son he loves, in whom we have redemption, the forgiveness of sins" (Colossians 1:13-14, NIV). But our transformation into the likeness of Jesus takes time.

Much of the New Testament is written to show us how to grow in faith and character; to believe God in good times and bad; to say, "No" to the world, the flesh, and the devil; and say, "Yes!" to God's presence, power, and purposes. Like a child growing up and becoming more mature, caring, and responsible, spiritual growth happens in much the same way. In his second letter, Peter reminds us of our faith's anchor:

> *His divine power has given us everything we need for a godly life through our knowledge of him who called us by his own glory and goodness. Through these he has given us his very great and precious promises, so that through them you may participate in the divine nature, having escaped the corruption in the world caused by evil desires.*
> *—2 Peter 1:3-4 (NIV)*

By grace, we "participate in the divine nature." Isn't that incredible? Then Peter describes spiritual growth, from giving up obvious sins to representing Jesus's love, compassion, and kindness to those around us:

> *For this very reason, make every effort to add to your faith goodness; and to goodness, knowledge; and to knowledge, self-control; and to self-control, perseverance; and to perseverance, godliness; and to godliness, mutual affection; and to mutual affection, love. For if you possess these qualities in increasing measure, they will keep you from being ineffective and unproductive in your knowledge of our LORD Jesus Christ.*
> —vv. 5-8 (NIV)

But Peter's description comes with a reminder to avoid thinking that we can grow through the sheer act of the will. Through it all, we keep depending on God's grace and power: "But whoever does not have them is nearsighted and blind, forgetting that they have been cleansed from their past sins" (2 Peter 1:3-9, NIV).

Did you catch that? If you aren't growing (or you aren't growing as fast as you'd like), remember the cross. Don't be "nearsighted and blind." Remember what Jesus has done for you and in you. Let His cleansing love motivate you to enjoy Him and please Him in everything you do.

MORE WAITING THAN YOU THINK

Luke's account of the early church seems like a whirlwind of activity. He tells us about Pentecost, Peter's sermon and 3,000 conversions, arrests and accusations, the stoning of Stephen, and the open door to the Gentiles through Cornelius. The second half of this history centers on Paul, and again, we see him going from city to city, seeing many come to faith, and being persecuted and tortured. A closer look, though, shows that Paul spent far more time waiting than working. In his biography of Paul, New Testament scholar N. T. Wright explains that in the roughly thirty years from meeting Jesus on the road to Damascus until his execution under Nero, Paul spent about three years in Arabia before he returned to Damascus and Jerusalem. After brief meetings there, he went home to Tarsus, in what is now southern Turkey, for ten years. During this time, he undoubtedly waded through the Scriptures to formulate the doctrines he would teach for the rest of his life. Barnabas traveled there and brought Paul back to Antioch. The Spirit sent the two missionaries on their first journey to Galatia, and then back to Jerusalem for the council that decided if Gentiles like us had to become Jews before we could be Christians (the good guys won!).

Paul took a new partner, Silas, on his second mission, this time all the way to Greece. He returned to Jerusalem for a short time and then took his third trip to raise money for the Christians in Jerusalem who were suffering a famine. When he returned to Jerusalem, he was arrested and imprisoned there and in Caesarea for two years.

He appealed to Caesar to hear his case, so he was sent by ship to Rome, where he was under house arrest for perhaps two more years. We don't know what happened to him after he was released, but he was arrested again, maybe two years after that. He was probably killed during Nero's persecution in about 64 AD. In these thirty years, Paul spent thirteen years in self-imposed exile in Arabia and Tarsus, perhaps two years in prison in Ephesus, and seven years under guard in Jerusalem, Caesarea, and Rome—a total of twenty-two years on the sidelines for one reason or another.[22] If you take away time for his traveling between cities by foot or by sea, he probably spent no more than six or seven years in direct ministry.

Paul trusted that God would use everything that happened for good. His letter to the Christians in Philippi is full of thanksgiving, though he was in prison at the time. He was glad that others were preaching the gospel, even if it was out of jealousy. He explained that God was using his imprisonment, ironically, to advance the cause of Christ. And he gave them additional perspective about suffering, providing context to a well-known passage:

> *But I rejoiced in the Lord greatly that now at last your care for me has flourished again; though you surely did care, but you lacked opportunity. Not that I speak in regard to need, for I have learned in whatever state I am, to be content: I know how to be abased, and I know how to abound. Everywhere and in all things, I have learned both to be full and to be*

---
22 N. T. Wright, "Paul: A Biography," The Third Well, https://www.thirdwell.org/paul-a-biography.html.

> hungry, both to abound and to suffer need. I can do all things through Christ who strengthens me.
> —Philippians 4:10-13

Why did Paul trust God in this long, convoluted process? Because he wanted what God wanted. His original agenda (being a top Pharisee and crushing the new Jesus movement) had been drowned in God's grace and purpose. When we try to rush the process and speed God up, we create problems instead of solving them.

> **WE HATE TO WAIT, BUT IT'S AN INTEGRAL PART OF HOW GOD REFINES OUR MOTIVES AND PREPARES US FOR THE NEXT STEP.**

I mentioned in an earlier chapter that God has tables prepared for us where we sit with other believers and pursue God's purpose and promise. Together, we enjoy the feast of salvation and encourage each other to "excel still more." Some of us look over at other tables and see people with a higher status in a company or church, a newer and nicer car, a bigger house, more luxurious vacations, and yes, a better bass boat, and we want to get up and sit with them before God tells us to move. Abram and Sarai thought they knew better than God about how His promise would be fulfilled, so they rationalized his relationship with Hagar, but Ishmael wasn't God's plan. They desired a promised table so badly, they created a provisional one, and it brought them heartache, compounding their anxiety over waiting for the promise.

When I compare myself with others in business or ministry, it always produces one of the twin evils of inferiority (if I'm not doing as well) or superiority (if I think I'm doing better). Neither of these is "loving others as you love yourself." I need to value the table where God has put me, draw from the wisdom of those sitting with me, and pour into their lives as well. When and if God wants to move me to a different table, I want to be surprised!

We hate to wait, but it's an integral part of how God refines our motives and prepares us for the next step. If we learn to wait expectantly, we'll find contentment while God works in us. It's not easy, but it's crucial. We say, "Yes!" not only to the next activity but also to times of waiting. Many years ago, Gregory of Nyssa said that his friend Basil had "ambidextrous faith" because he took the blessings of God in one hand and life's heartaches in the other, trusting God to use both to equip him to accomplish His will.[23] I want that kind of faith. I *need* that kind of faith.

---

23 Gregory of Nyssa, cited by Philip Yancey in *Reaching for the Invisible God* (Grand Rapids, MI: Zondervan, 2000), 69.

The answer to God's promise occasionally happens in an instant, but even then, there have probably been months or years of preparation, waiting patiently and expectantly for God to come through so that He gets all the glory. Settle in, and wait expectantly.

THINK ABOUT IT

CHAPTER 5

! Look at Psalm 130:5-6. How did the watchmen feel in the hour before sun up? How did they feel in the hour after it came up? What can we learn from them about waiting on God?

! What are some reasons many people hate to wait? How about you? What bugs you about waiting?

! What are some lessons God wants to teach us in the long, slow process of spiritual maturity? Which ones can't be learned in a hurry?

! What do you think it means to wait for the Lord "like the watchman waits for the morning"?

! Does it surprise you that Paul spent so much time out of action? (It surprised me!) What do you think he was doing while he was in Arabia, Tarsus, and in prison several times?

! On a scale of 0 (not at all) to 10 (all day every day), how often do you have "ambidextrous faith"? Explain your answer. What needs to happen to move the needle a few notches toward 10?

CHAPTER SIX

BELIEVING FOR THE UNBELIEVABLE

But Jesus looked at them and said to them, "With men this is impossible, but with God all things are possible."
—Matthew 19:26

For a reason I don't understand, a number of retired pastors started attending Encounter Church. When I noticed how many were coming, I asked the Lord, "What do You want me to do with all these people?"

He replied, "Just love them. Shepherd the shepherds."

Some of my pastor friends asked, "Doesn't it make you nervous to preach in front of all those preachers?"

I told them, "No, I'm not nervous. I'm preaching from the Bible. I'm not preaching heresy that makes me wonder if they'd be out to get me."

> **I'M NOT AGAINST CONFIRMATION, BUT I'M AGAINST EXCUSES AND PASSIVITY.**

One day, the Holy Spirit spoke to me: "I want you to rent a hotel and invite pastors to come for a retreat. I want you to love on them."

I told a friend about this plan, and he told me he'd been thinking about it too. I said, "God doesn't want you to just think. He wants you to do." I wasn't trying to offend him. I was just sharing what I've learned from God.

A lot of us get a word from God, but respond like Gideon, putting out fleeces to test the Lord to see if He really means it. I'm not against confirmation, but I'm against excuses and passivity. Like the parents of kids who are slow to obey, I think God gets frustrated when He gives us directions, but we find convenient excuses to delay action.

I told my friend, "I'm going to move forward with what God told me to do for pastors, and I'd love for you to join me."

He did. He sent me a list of ideas for a title for the twenty-four hours we would devote to the pastors and their spouses. One of them was "The One Day Sabbatical." I wanted to give them enough time to feel known, loved, and refreshed, but not take too much time out of their busy schedules.

We needed a place to stay and meet. A lady in our church told me about a hotel in Floyd, Texas she managed. I went to check it out. I drove past the little town and out into the country. Did I have the right address? Then I saw it . . . in the middle of a cornfield: a three-floor, forty-eight room hotel built like hundreds (or maybe thousands) of others around the country. I asked her what she would charge us to rent all the rooms for one night, use the large meeting room, and eat breakfast. When we added everything, from those costs to all of the other expenses, the total came to about $15,000.

I prayed, "Lord, how am I going to raise that kind of money to minister to pastors?" We weren't digging wells in Africa, and we weren't building an orphanage in South America. This was an event for pastors, which surfaced a significant problem: some people are "church hurt," but many more are "pastor angry." I'd heard enough stories of people saying, "When I was hurt and needed compassion, my pastor told me, 'Build a bridge and get over it!'" They see pastors as the problem, not the solution, so they weren't going to give to this effort. Still, God's directions were clear.

In March of 2022, I went on social media with the announcement: "If you're a pastor and you need to rest, a time to be refreshed, my wife Tracy and I would love to provide that for you. Give us twenty-four hours of your time. We're calling it "The One Day Sabbatical," and we hope you and your spouse will come. You don't know us, and we don't know you, but that's okay because the Lord knows who you are. Give us a day to let us love on you. It's completely free. All you need to do is get there." I gave the location and the dates and asked them to RSVP.

On faith, we booked the entire hotel.

I told our church what we were doing, and they stepped up. I explained, "We can spend $15,000 reaching the lost, and we'd see fruit from that effort. Or if we were part of healing and inspiring forty-eight pastors and their spouses, they would reach far more people and love them into the kingdom." Some of the people at Encounter Church gave thousands, many gave hundreds, and before I could blink, we had all we needed.

When they arrived, people from our church who had taken a day off work served the couples from the moment they got out of their cars. We carried their luggage into the hotel and to their rooms. We even carried their Bibles and everything else they brought with them. We provided several titles of popular, powerful books and invited them to pick any one they wanted. We fed them dinner the first night and breakfast and lunch the next day, and we had coolers with every type of soda and water. We even had some RC Cola and Big Red—the flavors of the Lord (besides Dr. Pepper, of course). We gave them hats and shirts to remember our time together.

Some of the couples were wary from the very beginning. They wondered when we were going to pull out our Amway spiel or invite them to buy timeshares. After a while, they realized this wasn't a bait-and-switch, so they relaxed and drank in the love we gave them. A few people shared important things they were learning about rest, refocus, and re-engagement, but we also provided times when they could share their hearts—their hurts and hopes—with each other.

When we started the twenty-four hours, the Lord told me to ask them to write the answer to a question: "What's the one thing you need that would make your life better?" They filled out their cards and turned them in to us.

When I read them, I prayed, "Lord, what am I going to do with all these?"

He replied, "You're going to meet their needs."

I protested, "In less than twenty-four hours?"

I sensed God saying, "Just trust Me."

That night, I went back to my room and began reading the cards and praying. One of them said, "I've been in ministry for many years, but my wife and I have never had any kind of special anniversary trip."

Tracy and I had a timeshare, so we decided to meet this need that way. Done. "That was easy, Lord."

Another read, "I need a soundboard, a Berenger X-32."

I had no idea how I could raise the money to buy this specific soundboard in a few hours the next day. I put this request in a pile that was for ones I didn't know how to answer.

One by Pastor Sam read, "My wife Chasidy and I are pastors and work for a mission. We've never had a home of our own. We'd like to have one someday."

Earlier that evening, before the first session, a man from the church approached me and said, "Pastor, I believe the Lord told me to give you this check today. It's $12,000. I don't know what it's for, but the Lord keeps putting housing on my heart." He handed the check to me. At the time, I didn't know what it was for, either.

When I read the request that night, I knew exactly what the check was for! It was for a down payment on a house for this couple. I put it in the "Done" pile.

In our last session together, I told people how God had answered their requests and met their needs. Many of them had written that they needed even more time to get away and be refreshed, so we spontaneously launched "The Pastors' Refuge," which would go from a Monday afternoon to Thursday morning. Twenty of the forty-eight couples received invitations to these retreats.

One pastor wrote that he needed a guitar, and it was provided. Another wanted help getting their church established on social media. We were blessed by Reach Right Studios to offer free help obtaining a Google Grant for nonprofits worth up to $10,000 a month in online marketing.

I told them that Pastor Phillip needed a soundboard, and we were working on getting one for him. Pastor Adam spoke up and said, "We have a Berenger X-32. Will that work?"

Phillip said, "Yes! That's exactly what we need!"

"It's at our church in Abilene. Where do you live?" asked Adam.

Philip replied, "Abilene."

Adam asked, "What's the name of your church?"

"Key City Church," Phillip told him.

Adam took a few seconds to gather himself, and then he explained, "God has been putting the name 'Key City' on my mind over and over the last few weeks. So much that I thought He was wanting me to change our church name to Key City Church. I didn't know what He meant . . . until now."

I started crying, and others in the room cried. I asked Pastor Sam and Chasidy to come to the front and tell the rest of the group about their ministry. They described their street ministry with homeless people, mostly addicts, in Dallas. They talked about providing meals, showers, shelter, and job opportunities. They were caring for "the least of these" in the city.

I asked, "What was the request you wrote on the card last night?"

Pastor Sam told the group, "Our mission provides enough funds for us to pay for an apartment, but we'd love to have a home. I have no idea how that might happen, but that's what I wrote on the card."

They had no idea what was about to happen. By this time, both of them were crying.

I said, "The Lord always provides for His children. He knows what we need before we ask. Yesterday, a man in our church handed me a check for $12,000, and he said the Lord had put 'housing' on his heart. He told me to use it in any way God led me to. We're passing it on to you for a down payment on a home."

> **WHATEVER YOU CAN BELIEVE GOD WILL DO, HE'LL DO, AND WHATEVER YOU CAN'T, HE'LL DO FOR SOMEONE LIKE ME WHO DOES.**

The place blew up. If people had been sniffling with a few tears before this moment, the floods came now! Some were kneeling, others had their hands in the air, and some came forward for prayer. I went to the keyboard and began singing Brandon Lake's "Gratitude"—It is truly overwhelming knowing all you have to offer is a Hallelujah when you see God do things ONLY GOD can do.[24]

The Holy Spirit fell on that place. It was one of the most beautiful moments I've ever experienced. Later that day,

---
24 Brandon Lake, vocalist, "Gratitude" by Benjamin William Hastings, Brandom Lake, and Dante Bowe, released 2020, track 3 on *House of Miracles*, Bethel Music Publishing.

after everyone had left and we finished packing up, I was exhausted but absolutely thrilled. God had done the spectacular . . . the unbelievable. I thought, *This is what happens when we say "Yes!" to God.* He led us to a hotel that was completely available for the one night we needed it. He led forty-eight couples to trust us enough to come. He provided all the money we needed from generous people who love Him. He met with each person at their point of need. And He answered our prayers for heart connections and meaningful interactions.

God invites us to believe Him for the unbelievable. Let me put it another way: Whatever you can believe God will do, He'll do, and whatever you can't, He'll do for someone like me who does.

THE RV

Seeing God do the unbelievable is a thrill. I expect Him to come through when I trust Him for crazy things, and He does. Let me tell another story. A friend invited me to lunch, where he was meeting with three other ministry leaders.

Earlier that morning, the Lord told me, "Get an RV and put it at an RV park."

I thought, *We don't need an RV. We're a church, not a travel show!* But I've learned to do what God says, even when it doesn't make any sense to me. I told Him, "Okay, it's Your money. Come to think of it, we don't have enough money to buy one. Just send me the right direction. I'm saying, 'Yes!'"

At lunch, the Holy Spirit told me to tell the missionary, "The Spirit told me to give you some money today."

He was very grateful (and both of us were surprised).

That afternoon, I called my buddy Carter, who is now the Executive Pastor at the church, and asked where he parks his RV. He told me it was at the Royce City RV Park. I asked my friend Keith, who invited me to lunch, if he wanted to check it out with me. As we were on our way to the RV park, I was all set to look foolish because I didn't own an RV. I envisioned this conversation:

"Excuse me, sir. I want to look at your available spots."

"How big is your RV?"

"Oh, I don't have one."

"Well, what are you planning to buy?"

"No clue. God told me to get an RV and put it at an RV park."

"Uh, okay. I assume this is for you and your family."

"Not that I know of. I don't know who will use it."

I played all this out on the drive to the RV park. I was sure I'd look like I'd lost my mind.

On the way, I got a call from a man in our church. He said, "Pastor, it's the strangest thing. I bought an RV four months ago, and this morning when I was praying, the Lord told me to call you and do with it whatever He put on your heart."

I told him about God speaking to me that morning, and we were both amazed. I didn't feel like I should ask him to give it to the church, so I asked, "How much do you want for it?"

He remarked, "Well, I don't know. It's only four months old." He paused for a few seconds and then asked, "Do you mind if I pray about it?" No problem.

I had directions to the RV park, but I couldn't find it. We drove past it before we saw the entrance. It was a secluded place in a pastoral setting with big trees with graceful limbs. Sheep were grazing on the grass between the RVs! I told my friend, "Oh man! This is the place. We're the sheep of His pasture!"

Later that afternoon, the man who owned the RV called to give me his price. He began, "Pastor, the RV is worth about $60,000." He couldn't hear me gulp. "But I'll let you have it for what I owe on it."

I said a quick prayer, "Lord, I sure hope he put up a big down payment!"

He said, "I owe $12,000."

I told him, "We'll take it."

I was thrilled . . . until I realized I didn't have $12,000. I prayed, "Lord, I don't have the money."

He responded, "I do. I didn't ask you to provide the funds. I only asked you to be obedient and say, 'Yes!'"

That same day, I shared the story with one of the church elders during an impromptu Wednesday night prayer service. He replied, "Pastor, I want to give $1,000 in honor of Benjamin, the least of the tribes of Israel."

I didn't tell him, but I didn't care if he was giving it for the tribe of the Choctaw Nation! I was just thankful for his generosity.

The next day, I got a letter from a couple who watch us online. The letter included a check for $5,000. The note said, "Pastor, we want to sow this into Encounter Church. Use it any way God leads you."

I prayed, "Lord, that's half."

I sensed the Lord say, "You have $6,000 in surplus in the church bank account. Use that for the rest of the payment for the RV."

Two weeks earlier, when I had looked at the account, I thanked God for the surplus and prayed, "Lord, I'm glad to have that extra money, but it's Yours. I know it's for something. Just let me know." So . . . when He said to use the surplus for the RV, I was ready.

I called the guy who owned the RV park and told him I was ready to talk about the price of one of his spaces. I explained that pastors come to our church and need a place to stay, and that's why we bought the RV. It's our version of an Airbnb, but at no charge to ministers and their families. He was impressed. He explained, "My mom and dad used to have missionaries stay at our house for six months at a time, so I totally get what you're doing." The space normally went for $500 a month, but he let us have it for a small fraction of that price. Now we had a paid-off RV and an almost free space for it in a beautiful setting—peaceful, quiet, with sheep grazing all around it.

When The Pastors' Refuge grew, we moved the RV to the ranch, where our guests hunt deer, wild turkey, and hogs for free. I field dress any animal they harvest. Tracy and I cook for them and serve them. They sometimes bring their children to hunt for the first time.

I often think back on God leading us to buy that RV. Many men and women of God have been blessed to stay in it and be refreshed.

A SICK WOMAN AND A DEAD LITTLE GIRL

The disciples saw Jesus do many things that seemed unbelievable. In one section of Luke's account of the life of Christ, they were crossing the Sea of Galilee when a huge storm threatened to sink the boat. The men, even the fishermen (maybe *especially* the fishermen), feared for their lives, but Jesus was asleep. They woke Him in a panic, and He stilled the storm and the waves (See Matthew 8:23-27). (In case you didn't know it, waves in a storm keep going long after winds cease, but Jesus brought calm to both in an instant.)

When they reached the other side, they were in Gentile country, where they saw a man who was possessed by "a legion" of demons. Jesus commanded them to come out of the man and enter a herd of pigs. The pig farmers weren't too happy with the trade of their pigs for the freedom of a man who had been tormented, so they asked Jesus and the disciples to leave (See Matthew 8:28-34). (On a side note, I'm pretty sure they ate well the next few days.)

When they sailed back to Capernaum, a crowd greeted them on the beach. Jairus met him there and begged Jesus to come to his house to heal his dying daughter. Jairus was a synagogue official, which gave him status in the religious and civic aspects of the life of the town. Jesus agreed to go with him, but on the way, a huge crowd jostled all around Him. Suddenly, Jesus felt something: power had gone out from Him. He looked down and saw a woman who had touched the hem of His robe. She had been bleeding for twelve years and spent all she had on doctors, but none of them could help her. But the touch of Jesus healed her (See Matthew 9:18-26).

In the middle of the crowd, with Jairus eager to take Jesus to his house, Jesus stopped to talk to the woman. They must have talked quite a while, because Luke tells us about a dramatic moment: "While [Jesus] was still speaking, someone came from the ruler of the synagogue's *house*, saying to him, 'Your daughter is dead. Do not trouble the Teacher'" (Luke 8:49).

Other Jewish leaders had been wary of Jesus, and many had fiercely opposed Him, but Jairus risked his reputation to ask Jesus to heal his daughter. Now, she was dead. Jesus had spent too much time with a sick woman instead of rushing to the bed of the child. It didn't make sense to Jairus, and it doesn't make sense to ER doctors today. In triage, you always take the critically ill patient first and let the chronically ill patient wait a little longer. When the ambulance sirens were blaring on the street to Jairus's house, Jesus had stopped to pay attention to someone who could have waited. At least, that's what would have been going on in my mind at that moment.

> **WHEN WE BELIEVE GOD WILL DO A MIRACLE, HE SOMETIMES TAKES US TO A DEAD END BEFORE HE OPENS THE FLOODGATES OF HEAVEN.**

Jesus overheard the man's tragic news and told Jairus, "Do not be afraid; only believe, and she will be made well" (Luke 8:50).

How would you have responded in that moment? Would you give up in heartache and anger, or would you believe Jesus for the unbelievable? Luke doesn't tell us that Jairus said anything, but Jesus followed him to his home. Jairus was (literally) taking steps of faith.

When they arrived, the rituals of mourning had already begun. People were weeping. Jesus told those who had assembled to comfort the parents, "Do not weep; she is not dead, but sleeping" (Luke 8:52). The mourners knew the little girl was dead, so they mocked Him.

In the girl's room, Jesus took the girl by the hand and said, "Little girl, arise" (Luke 8:54). It was the message spoken to little girls every morning in every culture by their loving parents, something like, "Honey, it's time to get up." The girl came back to life, and Jesus asked the parents to give her something to eat. (I guess being dead makes you hungry.) For Jesus, raising a dead girl to life is no harder than healing a sick woman. His power can do anything.

On the street during those long, torturous minutes while Jesus delayed, Jairus must have been incredibly anxious. Then, when he heard that his daughter was dead, he could have given up on Jesus. But he didn't. He still believed Jesus would do the unbelievable.

When we believe God will do a miracle, He sometimes takes us to a dead end before He opens the floodgates of heaven.

RESTORED

Sometimes, believing God for the unbelievable is about the depth and breadth of His forgiveness: Will He really forgive *that* sin? At the Last Supper, Jesus told His disciples again that He would be betrayed, arrested, and killed. Peter protested, "Lord, I am ready to go with You, both to prison and to death" (Luke 22:33). We know what happened. Jesus told him that he would betray Him three times before the night was over. Hours later, in Gethsemane, Jesus was arrested. True to his word, Peter stepped in to defend Jesus, swinging a sword and cutting the ear off the high priest's servant. (He was a fisherman, not a soldier, so he hadn't practiced his aim.) Most of the disciples ran for their lives, but Peter followed Jesus to the home of the high priest, where the Jewish rulers were prepared to host a private, illegal court to try Jesus.

It was cold that night, so Peter stood nearby next to a charcoal fire. A servant girl identified him, but he denied knowing Jesus. Two others noticed him, but he denied Jesus again. Luke takes us to that poignant scene: "Immediately, while he was still speaking, the rooster crowed. And the Lord turned and looked at Peter. Then Peter remembered the word of the Lord, how He had said to him, 'Before the rooster crows, you will deny Me three times.' So Peter went out and wept bitterly" (Luke 22:60-62).

Peter, the leader of Jesus's disciples, had failed miserably. Instead of being courageous, he chickened out. Jesus had told him, "On this rock I will build My church" (Matthew 16:18), but how could that happen now? It was over . . . all over.

The next day, Jesus was beaten, whipped, and crucified. He was put in a tomb, and His followers grieved. They went to bed that night sure that the worst thing in the history of the world had happened. They didn't realize His sacrifice for sins was the very best thing that ever happened! When Jesus came out of the grave on resurrection morning, He made sure to invite Peter to join the other disciples to meet Him in Galilee.

Jesus appeared several times over the next few weeks, and one of them was particularly meaningful for Peter. Several of the disciples went fishing on the Sea of Galilee. They fished all night but didn't catch any fish. The next morning at sunrise, they saw a man on the shore who told them to cast their nets again. They caught a lot of huge fish, and Peter remembered his first encounter with Jesus when the same thing happened. Peter recognized the man was Jesus, and he jumped into the water to swim to Him.

Jesus had prepared breakfast for them over a charcoal fire. After eating, Jesus asked Peter three times, "Do you love me?"

Each time, Peter replied, "Yes, Lord; You know that I love You." The third time, Peter obviously realized Jesus was asking three times because he had denied Him three times. But there was one other significant feature of this encounter. Experts say that smell is one of the strongest memories. The aroma of the charcoal fire on the beach at breakfast reminded Peter of the three denials when he stood next to a charcoal fire. Jesus wasn't shaming Peter. He was saying, "I want you to remember the worst thing you've ever done so you'll experience My forgiveness all the way to the bottom." The charcoal fire on the beach and the three questions were marks of great grace. Peter may have thought forgiveness and restoration were beyond comprehension—beyond believable—but Jesus made sure he understood and experienced the wonder of grace (See John 21:1-17).

EVEN THEM, EVEN ME, EVEN YOU

Jeremiah is known as "the weeping prophet" because he represented God during the dark days of the Babylonian exile, and he felt the full weight of their distress. At one point, he was in prison, but the word of the Lord came to him: "Thus says the LORD who made it, the LORD who formed it to establish it (the LORD *is* His name): 'Call to Me, and I will answer you, and show you great and mighty things, which you do not know'" (Jeremiah 33:2-3). The "great and mighty things" were about the promise to return God's people to their homeland—not soon, but eventually. He relayed God's promise:

> *Behold, I will bring it health and healing; I will heal them and reveal to them the abundance of peace and truth. And I will cause the captives of Judah and the captives of Israel to return, and will rebuild those places as at the first. I will cleanse them from all their iniquity by which they have sinned against Me, and I will pardon all their iniquities by which they have sinned and by which they have transgressed against Me. Then it shall be to Me a name of joy, a praise, and an honor before all nations of the earth, who shall hear all the good that I do to them; they shall fear and tremble for all the goodness and all the prosperity that I provide for it.*
> **—Jeremiah 33:6-9**

What does believing God for the unbelievable look like?

Lost people are found.

When William was five years old, the doctors diagnosed him with a brain condition that required surgery. It wasn't the only one he and his parents endured. From then until he was sixteen, William had four more surgeries, each one leaving his head partially shaved, leaving him with huge scars. He didn't mind when he was five, but as a teenager, he endured the snide comments of his peers. He was already insecure, but their mocking hurt him deeply.

In high school, he started drinking to numb the emotional pain. By the time he was in college, he drank a quart of whisky, gin, or scotch every weekend. His binging didn't affect his grades. He graduated with honors and was accepted to law school. Some days, he was either so drunk or so hungover that he could barely make it to class, but he graduated and passed the bar.

As a young lawyer in an established firm, one of the partners drank with him every day. He got married, had a child, committed adultery, and was divorced, and he numbed the pain with more alcohol than ever. After two years, he remarried, but before long, his new wife had had enough of him coming home drunk every day. Amazingly, he was still an effective attorney, so he didn't lose clients or his job, but he was about to lose another wife. She insisted that he get help for his alcoholism.

William went to Alcoholics Anonymous for two years. He got sober, but he rejected any dependence on God, which is a cornerstone of the recovery model. He "went out" again, drinking as much as before. For five years, he got drunk virtually every day. When his marriage was close to collapse again, he decided to go back to AA. This time, he had a different sponsor, one who told him that the "Higher Power" was Jesus Christ, who paid the penalty for his sins and offered him a new life with power to fight the insecurity that had plagued him since childhood.

The change was remarkable, and everyone saw it. William was not only sober; he was kind instead of being a bully, generous instead of grasping for every dollar and honor, and faithful instead of irresponsible. He kept meeting with his sponsor and others who had found Christ through their recovery, and he became a spiritual leader who had (and still has) a profound impact on men and women who "hit rock bottom" but looked up to find Jesus.

Those who knew William years before marvel at the transformation. He gets up each day and immediately falls to his knees to express his love for Jesus and his dependence on God. The transformation seems unbelievable . . . except that it's genuine and consistent.

Wounded people are healed.

I've known many people who suffered traumas, sometimes from shattering moments like a car accident or the terror of combat, but often from childhood abuse or abandonment. I understand their struggles because I'm one of them. I was sexually abused by two people, one whom was my babysitter's brother when I was very young. He was the teenage son of people in our church, and it happened more than once. I felt helpless. Years later, when I told my dad, he said, "If I'd known, I would have killed him!"

When I grew up, I had to lean hard on the Lord to forgive them and grieve the hurts and the loss of security as a child. When one of them died, my first thought was, *I sure hope he was saved.* That response let me know I'd really forgiven him instead of harboring bitterness and wishing he'd suffer. I thought it was over, but the pain ran deeper than I imagined.

When Haley was sexually assaulted, the anger flooded back. I relived the pain of my past all over again, and to be honest, I wanted to kill the guy who assaulted her! I realized that our past is like layers of an onion. We can forgive and grieve one layer, but God may reveal another layer, so we go through the process again . . . and again. This doesn't mean our forgiveness was flawed in any way. It only means we hadn't yet gotten to the core.

Many of us don't believe we can be honest with God about our past wounds. We're afraid we'll come unglued, so we minimize ("It wasn't that bad"), we excuse ("She couldn't help it"), or we deny ("It didn't even happen"). These are quick fixes that don't deal with the internal devastation. I kept my secret for a long time, but when I told Tracy—and she didn't run away or laugh or ridicule—another layer of healing began. The psalmist promises:

> *He heals the brokenhearted*
> *And binds up their wounds.*
> *He counts the number of the stars;*
> *He calls them all by name.*
> *Great is our Lord, and mighty in power;*
> *His understanding is infinite.*
> **—Psalm 147:3-5**

Those who have been deeply hurt often don't believe they can ever be made whole. The idea seems unbelievable to them, but the power of the love of God, energized by the Spirit of God, and imparted by wise, mature people in the family of God, can work miracles in a broken heart. I know. That's what happened to me.

Broken families are mended.

Rachel wondered why she and Tyler weren't as close as they used to be. When she tried to have meaningful conversations, he found reasons to leave the room to do something "important." He became secretive about his computer, and her suspicions skyrocketed when he came to bed later and later each night. One night, she got out of bed and sneaked into the living room, where Tyler was on his computer. As she suspected, he was looking at porn and chatting with women who inflamed his misguided passions.

She blew up: "How can you look at this filth when your children are in their bedrooms only a few feet away and could come in at any moment? And how could you do this to me?"

Tyler didn't offer any excuses. He promised he wouldn't do it any longer. For a few months, he was more attentive and kind to Rachel and their children, but then he became distant and secretive again. When Rachel confronted him, he admitted he had fallen back into his sinful habit. This time, she insisted they go to a counselor, "or I'm leaving with the kids."

The next four months of weekly counseling—for each individually and for them as a couple—surfaced a lifelong pattern of Tyler's addiction to porn and occasional visits to strip clubs. It was worse than Rachel suspected, but the counselor continually pointed them to God's love, forgiveness, and power through Christ. Over the next six months, shattered trust began to be restored, communication was more honest than at any time in their marriage, and God worked the miracle of reconciliation. Today, the couple leads a group for couples whose marriages are on the rocks. They're paying forward the hope they've found in Jesus.

Wandering people are redirected.

Janice wasn't exactly wandering; she was sprinting to the top of her company. She was determined and driven. She earned promotions over her peers because she was willing to work nights and weekends, even though she had two children growing up, barely knowing their mother. Her husband, Sam, continuously tried to get her to rearrange her priorities, but his pleading only drove her to work harder to prove herself.

This went on for years until the strain finally caught up with Janice. Over several months, she experienced pounding headaches, intestinal disorders, and muscle aches, in addition to being short-tempered and irritable (even more than before). Janice was on the verge of burnout.

She had become so preoccupied with climbing to the next rung up the organizational ladder that her entire life was falling apart. Her symptoms grew worse, so she finally found time to see her doctor. He told her, "There's nothing wrong with you that a different purpose wouldn't solve." Janice looked at him like he'd spoken Martian, so he continued, "Look, Janice, your body is telling you that it's on overload. God didn't design it to cope with the pressure you're under. If you don't change your habits, you'll risk lasting damage to your physical health. And if you don't change your values and your priorities, your habits won't change. Don't settle for addressing the superficial. Go to the root. Deal with what's driving you so hard. That's your best and highest hope."

When Sam asked her how things went with her doctor's visit, Janice told him, "Fine. No problem. He thinks I work too hard, but he doesn't understand how important my work is."

"Maybe he understands better than you do," Sam responded.

Janice barked back, "What do you mean?"

"I mean you're so focused on your career that you're missing out on seeing our children grow up . . . and you're missing out on our marriage."

"I'm doing all this for you and the kids!" she insisted.

"No," Sam calmly told her. "It's all about you—your success, your power, your prestige."

Sam had told her similar things many times over the last three years since their second child was born, but she had ignored him until now. For some reason, her hard heart melted in this moment. All the drive, all the passion, all the late hours suddenly were revealed for what they were:

idols she had worshipped more than anything else in her life. Janice wept.

The next few weeks were some of the most difficult but liberating of her life. She began reading a book about God's purpose for His children, and she had wonderful conversations with Sam about what's most important to her, to them, and to God. Gradually, new habits developed. She left work when everyone else did, she didn't work on weekends, and she devoted herself to knowing and loving Sam and the children. She was passed over for a promotion, but she didn't care. That life was over. Most of all, she put Jesus on the throne of her heart, letting Him reorient her priorities and refresh her heart.

I believe a lot of Christians don't believe God for the unbelievable because they don't want to be disappointed if He doesn't come through. That's true. He may not come through the way we expected, but He always comes through to accomplish His purposes in His way in His timing.

Has God put something on your heart as you read this chapter? Why not go out on a limb and trust Him to do what only He can do? What's the worst that can happen? He may show you that your request needs some tweaking. You can handle that. He may delay the answer to purify your motives or prepare the situation for a greater blessing. That's not a problem. He may have something far different and far better for you. You can accept that, can't you? Jesus gives us a better understanding of the Father's heart:

> *If a son asks for bread from any father among you, will he give him a stone? Or if he asks for a fish, will he give him a serpent instead of a fish? Or if he asks for an egg, will he offer him a scorpion? If you then, being evil, know how to give good gifts to your children, how much more will your heavenly Father give the Holy Spirit to those who ask Him!*
> **—Luke 11:11-13**

In his book *Gentle and Lowly*, Pastor Dane Ortlund reminds us that Jesus longs to reveal himself to us in love and strength. We don't have to plead with Him to be kind and generous to us. It's His delight! He's praying for us—attentively, wisely, and powerfully—right now. Ortlund writes:

> *Christ's heart is a steady reality flowing through time. It isn't as if his heart throbbed for his people when he was on earth but has dissipated now that he is in heaven. It's not that his heart was flowing forth in a burst of mercy that took him all the way to the cross but has now cooled down, settling back once more into kindly indifference. His heart is as drawn to his people now as ever it was in his incarnate state. And the present manifestation of*

his heart for his people is his constant interceding on their behalf.[25]

The unbelievable to us is totally believable to God. He will do what we trust Him to do.

---

[25] Dane Ortlund, *Gentle and Lowly* (Wheaton, IL: Wheaton: Crossway, 2020), 79.

THINK ABOUT IT

CHAPTER 6

> **!** Look at Matthew 19:26. What have been (and maybe are now) situations in your life when you needed to hear Jesus's message?

> **!** What is a work of God that seemed unbelievable before it happened? Who trusted God that it would happen? How did it affect them?

> **!** How do you think you would have responded if you'd been Jairus when Jesus delayed and friends came to tell you that your daughter had died, but Jesus looked at you and said, "Just believe"?

> **!** Describe the way Jesus restored Peter. Why was it important to remind him of his greatest sin and failure?

> **!** Who do you know who is . . .
> . . . lost and needs Jesus to find them?
> . . . wounded and needs Jesus to heal them?
> . . . broken and needs Jesus to restore their families?
> . . . wandering and needs Jesus to redirect them?

> **!** What are some common excuses people give to avoid believing God for the unbelievable? Have you used any of these? Explain your answer.

> **!** What promises can you cling to as you trust God to do something amazing?

CHAPTER SEVEN

ON THE OTHER SIDE OF OBEDIENCE

"You are My friends if you do whatever I command you. No longer do I call you servants, for a servant does not know what his master is doing; but I have called you friends, for all things that I heard from My Father I have made known to you."
—John 15:14-15

It's easy to say, "Yes!" to God when the path is clear and the outcome is predictable, but we're called to obey even when nothing is clear or certain. Most of the time, we only grasp God's intentions on the other side of obedience.

THE PROSTITUTE AND THE KING

Let me take you back to a familiar story but with some important insights. We meet Rahab the prostitute when Joshua took God's people across the Jordan and spies went into Jericho to see what it would take to conquer the city. Some theologians believe she was about ten years old when Moses led the people out of Egypt... forty years earlier. An account from the Jewish Women's Archive explains:

> *The Rabbis describe how Rahab was ten years old at the time of the Exodus from Egypt. She engaged in prostitution during the forty years of the Israelites' wanderings in the wilderness, until the age of fifty. Since there was no prince or mighty one who did not visit Rahab the harlot, she was well acquainted with people's thoughts. When she reported to the spies who came to her house: "no man had any more spirit left because of you" (Josh. 2:11), she alluded to her professional knowledge of the dimensions of the people's fears, because their apprehension affected their vitality when with her.*[26]

If Moses and the people had believed Joshua and Caleb's report about the Promised Land and set out immediately, it would have taken about eleven to twelve days to reach it. During those forty years, Rahab may have been molested, grown up, made a lot of bad decisions, and become old (by their standards).

---

[26] Tamar Kadari, "Rahab: Midrash and Aggadah," *Jewish Women's Archive,* https://jwa.org/encyclopedia/article/rahab-midrash-and-aggadah.

When Joshua and the people arrived at the banks of the Jordan, it was at flood stage. They could have forded the river in other seasons, but now they needed a miracle of the Lord stopping the water upstream to let them cross on dry ground. Jericho was a fortified city, their first big obstacle. As Joshua looked at the city, a mighty warrior appeared to him. Joshua asked the obvious question, "*Are* You for us or for our adversaries?"

He responded, "No, but *as* Commander of the army of the LORD I have now come."

Joshua prostrated himself and asked, "What does my Lord say to His servant?"

The Commander told him, "Take your sandal off your foot, for the place where you stand *is* holy" (Joshua 5:13-15).

Does that sound familiar? It did to Joshua. I'm sure he heard Moses talk about meeting God at the burning bush when He gave him the same command. Do you think this moment bolstered Joshua's faith? (It may have terrified and encouraged him at the same time.)

If Rahab was fifty years old, that's the year of Jubilee, the year following seven cycles of sabbatical years when debts are forgiven, slaves are freed, and land goes back to the original owners. For Rahab, this was her personal year of Jubilee! Joshua may have assumed that defeating

Jericho was simply part of God's plan for the people to take the land, but it was more than that, and Rahab was at the center of the hidden purposes of God. No one knew it then, but God was going to do something incredible on the other side of Rahab's courageous obedience to hide the spies. She married a man named Salmon, and they had a son, Boaz. Boaz met a Moabite refugee named Ruth, and they had a son named Obed. He was the father of Jesse, the father of David, the head of the line of Davidic kings, leading to the ultimate King: Jesus the Messiah, King of all. The purposes and plan of God included a prostitute, the most unlikely person to have a place of honor in God's kingdom.

Who could have imagined what would be on the other side of Rahab's obedience? God knew the blessings He would pour out on her, and now we know.

OVER, AROUND, AND THROUGH

Joshua and his army looked at the stout walls of Jericho and prepared for battle. The walls of the fortress were huge and complex, the perfect defensive position. The lower city wall was made of stone, about twelve to fifteen feet high. The upper wall was built using bricks; it was six feet thick and more than twenty feet high. An earthen embankment separated the two walls and gave the defenders the advantage of being able to look down (and shoot down) on those who attacked them. The tower inside the wall was made of stone, almost thirty feet tall, with an internal staircase for the watchmen. We can visualize a cutaway of the defensive fortifications:

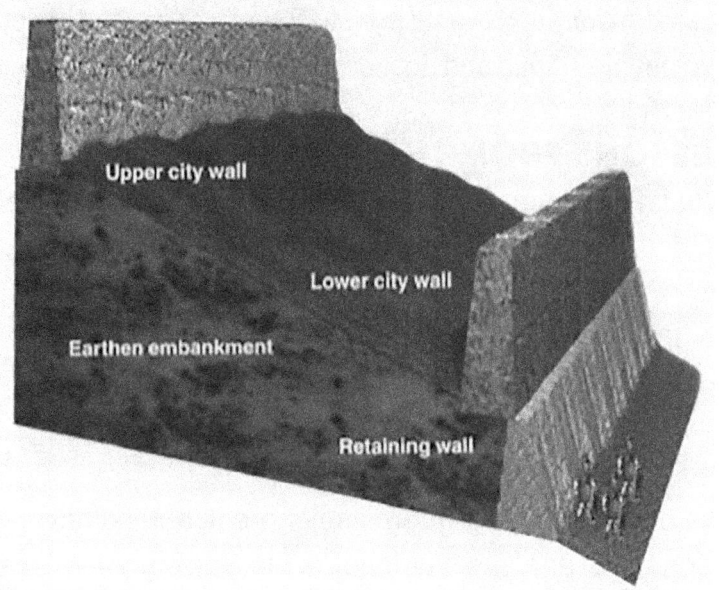

Joshua planned an assault, but God had other plans. You know the story. He told them to march around the city once a day for six days, with the army in front, followed by seven priests blowing rams' horns in front of the ark of the covenant. The people in Jericho probably thought they'd lost their minds. Then, on the seventh day, God told them to march around the city seven times. When they completed the last circle, Joshua yelled, "Shout, for the LORD has given you the city! Now the city shall be doomed by the LORD to destruction, it and all who *are* in it. Only Rahab the harlot shall live, she and all who *are* with her in the house, because she hid the messengers that we sent" (Joshua 6:16-17).

The people shouted, the priests blew their horns, and the walls fell down flat. God's army attacked the city but made sure to escort Rahab and her family to safety. It was one of the most dramatic events in history, and it happened because two people, Rahab and Joshua, obeyed the Lord's command.

LESSONS FROM THE WALLS

What do we learn about the importance of immediate obedience when God gives us directives?

> 1. Each of us is called to the wall.

I've been given a kingdom assignment, and so have you. Each believer plays a unique role in God's grand plans to seek and save the lost and make disciples of all nations. You may not be called to vocational ministry, but I can assure you that you're called to full-time ministry. Paul reminded the Colossians, "And whatever you do in word or deed, do all in the name of the Lord Jesus, giving thanks to God the Father through Him" (Colossians 3:17).

> **THE LORD DIDN'T CALL ME TO UNDERSTAND. HE CALLED ME TO TRUST HIM.**

When God gives you your assignment, you'll probably think, *Good grief! The wall is too big, and I'm too small!* In fact, if you don't feel that way, it's probably an assignment you've crafted yourself instead of one given by Almighty God, who can do anything through those who trust Him. Be assured: He won't bring you to a valley that He won't bring you through. On the other side is something far bigger and better than you can imagine.

When God led me to plant our church, I had no idea we'd have three campuses only a few years after we started—especially when I was ready to quit early in this season! But I listened to Tracy, who listened to the Holy Spirit. During that year of obedience, God did amazing things.

Having multiple campuses was never on the radar. I knew some outstanding leaders who had pulled that off, but me? Not a chance . . . until God said, "Do it." We did, and He blessed us. The Lord didn't call me to understand. He called me to trust Him. On the other side of obedience, we have three campuses, God is changing lives, and I'm writing a book about the goodness (and the surprise) of God. When He first put it on my heart to write a book, I told Him, "Lord, I don't have anything to say."

He replied, "But I do. Write the book."

2. Listen carefully.

I decided to obey God's leading to write a book, and I had a flood of ideas. I wrote them down. I had a dream about the cover—it said "Yes!!!" in big, bold letters with three exclamation points. When I shared my book ideas with a friend, he said, "Chris, those are your chapter titles. You're halfway there! You've already done the hardest part." He was a little too optimistic about the progress, but I appreciated his encouragement.

I hate to say it, but that conversation happened long before I took steps to complete the manuscript. The Lord had to make it very plain: "Finish the book this year." That's why I'm working on it today.

3. Do what God says.

Most of us are brilliant, skilled, and experienced . . . in making excuses for inaction. "I'm too busy." "I'm too tired." "I'm not sure it'll work." "Somebody else would do it better." The list is endless. One of the most common I've heard is, "I need to wait until I get confirmation." Sometimes, that's legitimate, but when we get confirmation, we often say, "Maybe one more," and one more after that. Christian author Randy Alcorn puts his finger on the causes and consequences of delayed obedience: "Many of us have elected to adjust our consciences rather than our lives. Our powers of rationalization are unlimited. They allow us to live in luxury and indifference while others, whom we could help if we chose to, starve and go to hell."[27]

Some of us want more answers and more guarantees before we take a step of obedience. We claim we're just being wise and careful, and besides, it's our personality type! There's nothing wrong with being wise and careful as long as it doesn't keep you from responding to God in faith and obedience. And can I add: Delayed obedience is still disobedience. When you're told to go and do it now, "No" is not a response God wants to hear.

4. Share the good news.

When God comes through, tell everybody you know. Shout it from the housetops and whisper it to those nearby. Psalm 66 encourages us to tell people about God's blessings:

> *Make a joyful shout to God, all the earth!*
> *Sing out the honor of His name;*
> *Make His praise glorious.*
> *Say to God,*

---
[27] Randy Alcorn, *Money, Possessions, and Eternity* (Carol Stream, IL: Tyndale House Publishers, 2003), 410.

> "How awesome are Your works!
> Through the greatness of Your power
> Your enemies shall submit themselves to You. . . .
> Come and see the works of God;
> He is awesome in His doing toward the sons of men. . . .
> Come and hear, all you who fear God,
> And I will declare what He has done for my soul.
> I cried to Him with my mouth,
> And He was extolled with my tongue.
> **—Psalm 66:1-3, 5, 16-17**

Young Life is a Christian parachurch ministry for teenagers. At the end of their summer camps, where God has worked in many lives, they gather everybody for a "Say So." The leader invites the kids, "If God has done something remarkable in your life this week, say so." Student after student gets up to talk about the wonderful working of God in their lives—many to come to faith in Jesus, others repent of sin, some are healed of emotional wounds, and God directs others to a fruitful life. We can adopt and adapt this ritual in a "Say So" often when we meet.

5. Look for people to inspire.

It's my prayer that this book will inspire you to believe God for more, not by shaming you for any unbelief but by pointing you to the God of wonders and glory. When we get a better glimpse of Him, we don't need to pressure anyone to believe God for more. Faith grows in us and spills out of us into the lives of others. One pastor reminded us of God's faithfulness so we can remind others: "God will meet you where you are in order to take you where He wants you to go."

6. Enjoy a close relationship with Jesus.

Obedience doesn't earn closeness with God; our actions aren't a bargaining chip to get something we want. But our trust in God that produces obedience puts us in touch with His heart. When Jesus was walking with the disciples in the Garden before His arrest, He told them:

> *You are My friends if you do whatever I command you. No longer do I call you servants, for a servant does not know what his master is doing; but I have called you friends, for all things that I heard from My Father I have made known to you.*
> —John 15:14-15

OBEDIENCE IS OFTEN HARD, BUT DISOBEDIENCE IS DISASTROUS.

Isn't friendship with Jesus what your heart longs for? (I'm sure it is, or you wouldn't have read so far in the book.)

Let me put the principles of this chapter in perspective: Obedience is often hard, but disobedience is disastrous. Many of us live in heartache and shame because we didn't obey God. Obedience is a big challenge, but it results in joy, freedom, and impact. The good news is that God is a God of second (and third and fourth and . . .) chances. His forgiveness knows no bounds, and He can restore the years the locust has eaten (See Joel 2:25). If God had a wonderful plan for a prostitute, then no one is beyond His loving reach. All of us have been disobedient, and all of us have another opportunity to say "Yes!" to God.

Remember: You may feel inferior because you don't have degrees, but if you're still alive, you have a temperature.

THINK ABOUT IT

CHAPTER 7

> **!** Read John 15:14-15. What are some ways that obedience draws us closer to the heart of Jesus?

> **!** Joshua's assignment was to conquer Jericho, even though it had a strong wall. What is your "wall," your kingdom assignment? Is it clear to you? Why or why not?

> **!** Are you on the end of those who are quick to act (sometimes without much thinking) or on the other end of those who spend too much time analyzing before they act (if they ever do)? Explain your answer. Is any change needed?

> **!** What are some ways to determine if an impression is from God or just the result of last night's pizza?

> **!** What answers to prayer and wonderful works of God can you tell people about right now? What prayer is yet to be answered?

> **!** Who are two or three people God has put in your life to inspire their faith? How well are you inspiring them now? What habits can you incorporate to do it better?

CHAPTER EIGHT

YOU HAVE MY "YES!!!"

But be doers of the word, and not hearers only, deceiving yourselves.
—James 1:22

I hope the title of this chapter isn't just words on a page to you but the cry of your heart. Because you grasp the wonder of God's grace poured out on you through Jesus, you want to honor Him in everything you think, say, and do. You don't have to wait for God to speak to you for you to say, "Yes!" because He's already spoken loudly and clearly through His Word.

Does God want you to respond to His limitless love by loving Him in return? Yes!

Does God want you to love the unlovely? Yes!

Does God want you to care for the hurting? Yes!

Does God want you to be kind to people who annoy you? Yes!

Does God want you to use every opportunity to share His love with others? Yes!

Does God want you to be generous with your time, talents, and treasure in response to His generosity toward you? Yes!

I could go on, but you get the idea. I want to speak to four groups of people:

- You may have developed a lifetime pattern of saying, "Yes!" to God. Fantastic! Keep it up. Encourage others to follow your example.
- You may remember a season of your life when you said, "Yes!" to Him, but you've drifted. He welcomes your return.
- You may be afraid to say, "Yes!" to God because you're not sure what it will cost you. Be assured that the blessings will far outweigh the costs.
- Or you may be saying, "Yes!" to Him for the first time at this very moment. Way to go! Jesus is smiling right now, and heaven is throwing a party.

For me, saying "Yes!" to God is like being addicted to cocaine. (Now, I want to add quickly that I don't know this from firsthand experience, but from what I hear from addicts, I can relate.) One hit makes you want another, and the second one redoubles your desire for the next one.

Before long, you can't imagine life without it. You're hooked ... this time, in a good way. I may not be the sharpest tool in the shed, but I've figured out that every time I obey God's directive and see Him come through, I can't wait to hear Him give me the next instructions. Addicts wake up every day thinking about how and where they can get their next hit. I wake up every day thinking about the adventure God has for me that day, and I can't get enough!

Do I have doubts and fears about my abilities and God's provisions? Yes, certainly. I often pray, "Lord, I don't know how I can do this." He always responds, "I'm not asking you to do it. I'm going to do it. Just trust Me and do what I tell you to do. Stand and see the salvation of the Lord."

Do you remember the first time you ate bacon? Didn't you want to eat it again? I don't know why God banned the Israelites from eating it. I think it's one of God's greatest blessings, and I look for it on every menu. I could say the same thing about pizza, rollercoasters, hunting, and fishing. Do kids mind climbing hundreds of stairs to the big slide at the waterpark? No, the thrill of the ride makes it worth the effort ... a dozen times in a row!

Saying "Yes!" to God is a rush, an emotional high given by the Most High.

I remember hearing Reinhard Bonnke share his testimony of God calling him to a life of evangelism. He asked, "God, why did You choose me?"

God told him, "You weren't my first choice, and you weren't my second choice, but you said, 'Yes!'"[28]

A while back, Chris Negron, the campus pastor at the Encounter Church Quinlan campus, and I attended a pastors' retreat in North Carolina. At the end, we were given an opportunity to visit the Billy Graham Museum. It has exhibits and videos about the great evangelist, including his humble beginnings. As I sat in the auditorium watching the first video, the Lord said to me, "You know, you're just like him."

I thought it was the enemy tempting my pride, so I rebuked the thought. I responded, "I'm not like him at all. Look at all he's done!"

Five seconds later, the video showed Billy Graham saying, "All I did was say 'Yes!' to the Lord."

God said, "I didn't say you've accomplished all he accomplished. I didn't say you will or won't accomplish as much. You're like him because you said, 'Yes!' to Me."

---

28 Don Finto, "Reinhard Bonnke," *Caleb Global*, 18 Dec. 2019, https://caleb.global/reinhard-bonnke/.

When you give God your "Yes!," you to see His best at work in your life.

I love the song lyrics, "All my life You have been faithful. All my life You have been so so good."[29] David said it like this: "

> *I have been young, and now am old;*
> *Yet I have not seen the righteous forsaken,*
> *Nor his descendants begging bread.*
> **—Psalm 37:25**

In the depths of national calamity in the Babylonian exile, Jeremiah found God to be faithful:

> *Because of the LORD's great love we are not consumed,*
> *for his compassions never fail.*
> *They are new every morning; great is your faithfulness.*
> *I say to myself, "The LORD is my*
> *portion;therefore I will wait for him."*
> *The LORD is good to those whose hope is*
> *in him,to the one who seeks him;*
> *it is good to wait quietly for the salvation of the LORD.*
> **—Lamentations 3:22-26 (NIV)**

If God is faithful to people in the most difficult situations in their lives, He will be faithful to you, too.

---

29 Bethel Music and Jenn Johnson, vocalists, "Goodness of God" by Jason David Ingram, Brian Johnson, Edmond Martin Cash, Benjamin David Fielding, and Jenn Johnson, November 15, 2019, track 12 on *Believe For It,* Puresprings Gospel.

OF TWO MINDS

God has demonstrated His love toward us by sending His Son to die the death we should have died and live the life we couldn't live. The Bible doctrine of justification has two parts: forgiveness and righteousness. Our sins created a debt to God, which deserved the ultimate punishment of separation from God, but Jesus's death was the complete payment for our debts. His last words were, "It is finished" (John 19:30), which means the debt has been satisfied. At that moment, the heavy, ornate, sixty-foot-high veil separating the Holy of Holies (where God dwelt with the ark) and the Holy Place (where you'd find the candlestick, the table for the showbread, and the altar of incense) was torn in two. Jesus's sacrifice paid it all, so the separation between God and man was ripped apart from top to bottom. Because we're completely forgiven, we have access to God's very presence!

> **WE CAN'T BE ANY MORE LOVED, FORGIVEN, AND ACCEPTED THAN WE ARE RIGHT NOW—NOT BECAUSE OF OUR PERFORMANCE BUT BECAUSE OF CHRIST'S PERFORMANCE.**

The second aspect of justification is imputed righteousness. No, our thoughts, words, and behaviors fall short of God's best, but because we're "in Christ," His righteousness has been credited to our account. When God looks at us, He sees the righteousness of Jesus. This means the Father warmly accepts us, so we have a relationship with Him as beloved, adopted sons and daughters.

Do you struggle with insecurity? Do you feel inferior (and perhaps try to cover it up by acting superior)? The Creator of the Universe, the God of Glory, considers you to be His treasure and His masterpiece (Ephesians 1:18 and 2:10). Do you worry that you don't belong? Your name is inscribed on God's hands (Isaiah 49:16).

We can't be any more loved, forgiven, and accepted than we are right now—not because of *our* performance but because of *Christ's* performance. Amazingly, the Father loves us as much as He loves Jesus, and Jesus loves us as much as the Father loves Him (John 15:9 and 17:23)!

I wanted to say all that before dropping the hammer. In spite of the wonderful, incredible, soul-nurturing, endearing truths of our identity as God's dear children, we're still flawed people who live in a fallen world, and it's easy for us to lose our focus. James warned believers in his day and ours:

> *If any of you lacks wisdom, let him ask of God, who gives to all liberally and without reproach, and it will be given to him. But let him ask in faith, with no doubting, for he who doubts is like a wave of the sea driven and tossed by the wind. For let not that man suppose that he will receive anything from the Lord; he is a double-minded man, unstable in all his ways.*
> **—James 1:5-8**

Double-minded. Wanting God *and* success, pleasure, and approval. Reading the Bible and praying, but not acting on what God says to us. Looking the part of a committed Christian, but hedging our bets by being stingy with our money and affection. Famous pastor E. Stanley Jones warned, "If you don't make up your mind, your unmade mind will unmake you."[30] How can you tell if you're a double-minded person? Thanks for asking. William Temple said that the test of our hearts is what we think about when we don't have to think about anything at all.[31] What fills the empty space? Is it the wonder of God's goodness and greatness and the opportunities to honor Him, or is it daydreams about acquiring prestige, winning the lottery, getting away from it all on a fabulous vacation, or getting even with someone who hurt you? I'm not suggesting that it's a sin to ever think about something other than God, but what dominates your thoughts?

---

[30] E. Stanley Jones, *The Way to Power and Praise* (New York and Nashville: Abingdon Press, 1959), 4.
[31] Yale Author, "Silence and Solitude," *Ichthus*, 13 March 2019, https://harvardichthus.org/2019/03/silence-and-solitude/.

> **GOD'S ANOINTING DESTROYS THE IDOLATROUS YOKE, AND GOD'S GLORY DESTROYS THE SELFISH AGENDA.**

We say, "Yes!" to something or someone every waking moment—even if it's indecision and inaction. It's easy to be yoked to comfort, acclaim, power, social media, control, the news, and any of a hundred other things. The reason I've gone to great lengths in this chapter to describe the power of God's grace to set us free and redirect our hearts to the things of God is that it's so stinking easy to let other things encroach on our passion for Jesus, watering it down until it's little more than window dressing for others to see when they walk past us. Here's the solution:

God's anointing destroys the idolatrous yoke, and God's glory destroys the selfish agenda.

The anointing is having a purpose in God's forever kingdom that transcends anything the world offers, and the glory captures and fills our hearts with wonder, so we want God to be the center of everything in our lives.

YOUR NEXT STEP

The only assumption I can make as we get to the last chapter of this book is that if you've read this far, God is working powerfully in you. He has prepared you for your next step, but your step may be different from those others will take.

Your "Yes!" may be to receive Jesus's offer of love and forgiveness.

Many people are "cultural Christians." When I asked one man if he was a Christian, he looked surprised and replied, "Well, I'm not a Hindu or a Muslim." Others assume that God grades on a curve, and if your good deeds outweigh your bad ones, you're heaven-bound. That's moralism, not the gospel of grace! Yes, good deeds are important, but the order is the experience of grace first . . . and then actions pour out of a heart full of gratitude.

Paul's letter to the Christians in Rome gives us a clear picture of God's grace: All of us are sinners who fall short of God's perfection, but "while we were still sinners" (Romans 5:8), Christ died to pay for our sins. If we confess with our mouths and believe in our hearts that Jesus is the Christ, we're rescued from sin, death, and hell. And then, as a response to all God has done for us and in us, we present ourselves to God as "living sacrifices" to please Him (Romans 12:1), which is the only reasonable response to the greatness of His grace, love, forgiveness, and power.

If you've believed that you had to be good enough to earn God's acceptance, I have great news for you: You can't! But Jesus can and did it for you. Trust Him to forgive you and transfer you into His kingdom.

Do you feel (or has someone told you) that you're disqualified because of your sordid past, your race, your sexual preference, or some other reason? Here's the truth: all of us were disqualified and unqualified, but faith in Christ changes everything. We're now secure, confident, and thrilled because Jesus did for us what we couldn't do for ourselves.

Jesus's offer is to everyone, including prostitutes, murderers, and self-righteous prigs . . . and including you. Take His hand and follow Him.

Your "Yes!" may be to rearrange your life around Him.

Baptism is a picture of new priorities. As we've seen, we're plunged into the water to identify with Jesus's death and burial, and coming out represents our new values, power, and purpose as those who have been made alive in Christ. We're baptized once, but we live the message of baptism every day. Paul wrote, "And do not be conformed to this world, but be transformed by the renewing of your mind, that you may prove what is that good and acceptable and perfect will of God" (Romans 12:2). We spend the rest of our lives focusing on what God wants to do in and through us. We want our lives to count and to make a difference to those under our roofs, in our neighborhoods, and around the world.

If you aren't sure what God's priorities are, read your Bible. They're listed and described on almost every page. If you want to focus on one part and camp out there, read Paul's letter to the Ephesians three or four times, and each time, ask, "What is God's agenda?" and "What in me needs to change so my heart and actions are in line with His agenda?" (If you can't see any differences, read it again.)

Your "Yes!" may be to repent of recurring sin.

I hope this book has convinced you that Christ's payment is sufficient for any sin, public or private, large or small. You may have a secret obsession that draws you away from God, or you might be a hitman for the mob. Nothing and no one are beyond the reach of God's cleansing flood!

Sinful habits form neural pathways just like deep hurts form them . . . or more positively, consistent experiences of love and constructive God-honoring habits form better pathways. Deeply rooted habits don't change easily, but they can be replaced by the truth of God's Word, the power of God's Spirit, and the encouragement and support of God's people.

Some church traditions blast people with warnings about the consequences of sin. These leaders may mean well, but they can produce more fear than faith. Other traditions are on the other end of the stick: they seldom talk about sin and repentance, so their people become complacent about their sins. We need a better understanding.

When Martin Luther nailed his "95 Theses" to the church door at Wittenberg in 1517 to protest the church's practice of asking people to pay money for forgiveness, the first one on his list was: "When our Lord and Master Jesus Christ said, 'Repent' (Matthew 4:17), he willed the entire life of believers to be one of repentance."[32] The entire life? Yes, because, rightly understood and practiced, repentance reconnects us with the source of God's forgiveness, love, and strength . . . and we need that reconnection often and always!

There are actually two very different kinds of repentance. Paul describes them in his second letter to the Corinthians. One is based on shame; he calls it "the sorrow of the world." In this one, when we become aware of our sin, we beat ourselves bloody. We tell ourselves we're terrible, horrible people, and our solution is to feel bad enough long enough—which is a form of penance, not the experience of forgiveness. People who have this practice of repentance avoid it like the plague because it crushes their spirits and makes them feel terrible. Paul says it's a kind

---
32 "95 Theses," luther.de, https://www.luther.de/en/95thesen.html.

of death—death to joy, death to intimacy with Jesus, and death to security.

Thankfully, there's another kind. Paul wrote, "For godly sorrow produces repentance *leading* to salvation, not to be regretted" (2 Corinthians 7:10). He's not talking about the kind of salvation of becoming a Christian, but the daily kind of experiencing God's love and forgiveness even (maybe especially) when we sin. In this kind of repentance, we know we're forgiven because of Jesus, so we're not afraid to be brutally honest with God about our sin. When we confess and repent, we experience His love again, and we're more motivated than ever to honor Him. Paul saw the effects of this kind of repentance in the Corinthians believers: "For observe this very thing, that you sorrowed in a godly manner: What diligence it produced in you, *what* clearing *of yourselves, what* indignation, *what* fear, *what* vehement desire, *what* zeal, *what* vindication!" (2 Corinthians 7:11)

Do you see the difference? Worldly sorrow is shame, self-condemnation, and a barrier to the experience of God's grace. Godly sorrow is based on confidence in God's forgiveness, which restores and empowers us to live for Him.

Pick the right one!

Your "Yes!" may be to invite God to heal deep wounds.

Some might wonder why people are reluctant to ask God to heal emotional and relational wounds. The answer is that they hurt so much that even surfacing them is too painful. It's like being hurt all over again. It takes a lot of courage to start the healing process. Thankfully, God doesn't make us aware of the full extent of the wounds at first. We couldn't handle it! Instead, He gives us enough to grieve, forgive, and heal, and later, He shows us more.

We're wounded in relationships, and we're healed in relationships. One of the hardest things for many people is finding someone to trust so they can begin to tell their stories, but this connection is crucial. They can look for a pastor, counselor, or wise friend who has experience helping others cope with the most painful events in their lives. The process is messy. They can't expect instantaneous healing for deep and long-lasting pain, but God is faithful. He provides the right person to help, the right comfort and encouragement, and the right timing for each step in the process. For a few, the miracle of healing happens quickly, but for most, it's like healing a broken bone: it takes time, attention, and care.

I know the fears this "Yes!" generates, but I also know the healing, peace, and joy on the other side of obedience in this very personal and very vulnerable part of life. In Revelation, we get a glimpse of the cosmic struggle between the enemy and God. It's a fierce fight, but (Spoiler alert!) God and His people win in the end. At one point, the enemy seems about to overwhelm believers, but John tells us, "And they overcame him by the blood of the Lamb and by the word of their testimony, and they did not love their lives to the death" (Revelation 12:11). The blood of the Lamb freed us from the pit and gave us new life, and the word of our testimony drives that reality deeper into our hearts. Wonderful things happen when we share our stories with safe people: It frees us from the enemy using our secrets against us. God will turn it around and use it for good, causing us to grow stronger and wiser, and it shows others that they can trust God with their deepest hurts, too.

When God led me to share about being sexually molested when I was a boy, I was very reluctant. I prayed, "Lord, they won't want me as their pastor if they know this."

I was really nervous, but the Lord assured me, "Just share it."

That Sunday morning, I told the people, "I'm embarrassed to tell you something about my childhood, but the Lord told me to be transparent, so here goes." I told them about the two people who abused me, the threats by the enemy to keep me quiet, and the long healing process. I could tell people were paying close attention. Nobody moved a muscle. When I finished, a young lady stood up and asked, "Pastor, do you mind if I say something?"

How could I say, "No"? I motioned for her to speak. She walked up to the front, and I handed her a mic. She began,

"The same thing that happened to Pastor Chris happened to me." She said a few things about her experience, then she turned to me.

The Spirit gave me an idea. I asked her, "Will you sit with me as the service ends?" She nodded, and we sat together at the edge of the stage. I told the people, "If you've been a victim, I want to invite you to stand when we stand up. That will mean that you want to be a victor, an overcomer, and see God's healing hand in your life."

The young lady and I stood up . . . and over half of the congregation stood with us—young and old, men and women, all races, people from all backgrounds, rich and poor. I expected a few to stand, but not this many. I realized we'd been afraid to be vulnerable with each other for years. Now we were honest with God and each other, and He began to bring the light of healing and hope into the darkest recesses of our hearts. Talk about building community!

Your "Yes!" may be to pull the plug on comparison, competition, and resentment.

It's human nature to compare, but it's *fallen* human nature to do it so we can feel superior to others. We do it so often that we don't even realize it. It's like asking a fish, "How's the water?" The fish answers, "What's water?"

A friend told me that a woman in his church said she always sat in the front row, not to be closer to the band and the pastor, but to avoid comparing her hair to the women who sat in front of her during the services, like she did before she made the move.

Social media has made the problem worse, but it's been with us since the dawn of time. In Psalm 73, Asaph tells us about his experience with comparison. He was hopping mad that people who didn't even try to follow God lived better lives than he did, and he had been faithful to God. He obviously did a lot of complaining about his situation, because he spent a large section of the psalm griping that they had everything they wanted, but he kept coming up short. Finally, the Lord gave him insight into the situation: People will get what they deserve; God is just. Near the end of the psalm, Asaph looks back on his emotional distress when he was so full of self-pity and resentment:

> *When my heart was grieved and my spirit embittered,*
> *I was senseless and ignorant; I was a brute beast before you.*

Have you ever felt like that? I have, and you may have, too. Life doesn't seem fair, and you're mad! But in one of the most beautiful and tender turns in the Scriptures, Asaph tells us what God did:

> *Yet I am always with you;you hold me by my right hand.*
> *You guide me with your counsel,and*
> *afterward you will take me into glory.*
> *Whom have I in heaven but you? And earth*
> *has nothing I desire besides you.*
> *My flesh and my heart may fail,but God*
> *is the strength of my heart*
> *and my portion forever.*
> **—Psalm 73:23-26 (NIV)**

Did you catch that? When Asaph was at his worst, God took his hand, gave him wisdom about the future for him and "those people," and became more to him than all the wealth and comfort in the world. His conclusion? "And earth has nothing I desire besides you." That's what a "Yes!" (even one that comes on the backside of struggle) gets you. There's no compulsion to compare because our hearts are full and overflowing, so there's no competition with others who have more or less, and no resentment that God isn't fair.

Your "Yes!!!" may be to "that one thing" you've avoided for so long.

You may be successful in most areas of your life, but there's that thing—the one you hoped I wouldn't shine a light on. I don't know what it is, but you do . . . and God does. It's time. No more delays, no more excuses.

Years ago, when I was a youth pastor in Virginia, I felt God's leading to get into standup comedy. I thought, *That's crazy. People laugh a lot when I talk to them, but that's a long way from performing . . . in front of a crowd!*

At one point, we held a training seminar for youth pastors. One of my best friends, Chris, was there, and when it was over, we went to lunch. He has a prophetic gift and had given words to several people during the training. Kind of kidding, I said, "Hey, do you have a word for me, too?"

Instantly, he said, "Yes, I do." He put his fork down. "I've been waiting all weekend for you to ask me."

I thought, *Why do I need to ask if you have a word for me?* But I didn't say it.

Chris launched in: "God has been trying to get you to do something for two years. He put it on your heart, and people have said you'd be great at it, but you've dismissed it." He let that sink in for a few seconds, and then he continued, "The Lord has been opening doors for you—opportunities beyond anything you can imagine—and all you have to do is say, 'Yes!' to Him."

I knew exactly what he was talking about. God wanted me to do standup. Actually, I'd gotten a little confirmation just a couple of days earlier. I was at a store to buy a lightbulb for a microwave, and I was cutting up with the salesman.

He was laughing, and a lady in the next aisle overheard us, and she was laughing. The salesman told me, "Man, you ought to do standup!"

I said, "I am. Right now. I'm standing up waiting for you to find the bulb I need! Times a wastin', friend, and I am not getting any younger!"

After my friend's word, I had to take a step of faith. Our church was a serious, God-focused church with a strong sense of purpose and clear values. I hadn't read the bylaws very carefully, but I suspect hosting a comedy club wasn't mentioned anywhere. I looked at our church calendar, which was always packed with activities. A Friday night six weeks out didn't have anything scheduled. I explained to my pastor that I wanted to invite people so I could do comedy that night. He agreed, and I said, "I have one more request: Do you mind if I take an offering?"

He kind of frowned and asked, "What are you going to use the money for?"

"No, it's not for me," I began to explain. "I plan to record the event and make a live CD. I'll only use the money to cover the expense of the recording. If there's any more, I'll give it to the church or the youth group or wherever you want it to go."

He agreed, so I started planning the publicity, the seating, the recording, and, oh yeah, my routine. I was going to walk on the stage with a sign that said, "Will work for food." I weighed 125 pounds more than I do now, so I thought that would be a good beginning.

That night, 200 people showed up, and it went better than I expected. When I counted the offering, it was exactly the amount for the recording, to the penny. I had two CDs made, and I sent one to Chris. I figured he'd be a good sounding board, since he was the one who gave me the confirming word to move forward in this new ministry.

A few days later, Chris called. He said, "Man, is this the thing God was telling you to do? This is funny."

I replied, "Yes!"

He asked, "Would you come do standup at the grand opening for The Potter's House? It's going to be a huge morning and evening."

If you know what I said to him or at least feel like you do, you should say it out loud right now: "YES!" If you need proof of my "Yes!", you can find video evidence on YouTube by searching Chris Binion "Live at The Potter's House."

What's your "one thing"? What has God put on your heart that you've said, "No," or "Wait," or "I'm sure somebody can do it better"? It's time to say, "Yes!"

Your "Yes!" may be to step into service.

God didn't rescue you from sin and death to just sit for an hour on Sunday morning (or *some* Sunday mornings). We are children of our loving Father, citizens of His kingdom, and servants of the Most High. Each of us is part of the body, with Christ as the head. In his first letter to the Corinthians, Paul hammers the point that every part is crucial. You may be a toenail, but be the best one you can be. When people have an ingrown toenail, they suffer, and they're not as mobile as they could be. We need to be strong and healthy in every part.

> **WE'RE ALL IN FULL-TIME MINISTRY.**

We make a mistake in thinking that opportunities to serve are limited to the walls of our churches. We need to think bigger . . . much bigger. Ask God to lead you to a place where your heart connects with a need and then give it all you've got. Most of us need to experience some trial and error before we find the best fit. That's perfectly fine. Don't be discouraged. The right place is out there for you.

Before Jesus ascended to the right hand of the Father, He told His disciples:

> *All authority has been given to Me in heaven and on earth. Go therefore and make disciples of all the nations, baptizing them in the name of the Father and of the Son and of the Holy Spirit, teaching them to observe all things that I have commanded you; and lo, I am with you always, even to the end of the age.*
> **—Matthew 28:18-20**

This instruction wasn't just for the eleven listening to Jesus. It's the blueprint for a worldwide movement, one that requires all of us to play our part. Some would say the Great Commission has been fulfilled because the gospel is heard in every nation, but some in those countries haven't heard, many have heard something a half-step short of a clear gospel presentation, and besides, more people are born to every generation—so the Great Commission needs to be fulfilled continually.

We're all in full-time ministry.

Your "Yes!" may be to answer the kingdom assignment of vocational ministry.

God called me from a successful banking career to be a pastor. He called an executive in a national accounting firm to be the executive pastor of a one-year-old church plant. He called a young man who was accepted to law school to work in youth ministry. These and countless other stories make no sense to a lot of people, but they were saying, "Yes!" to God, not their parents, bosses, or friends.

> **YOU DON'T GET TO CARRY THE FIRE OF GOD IF YOU'RE NOT WILLING TO CARRY THE WOOD FOR THE SACRIFICE.**

Tracy and I had a plan for me to be bi-vocational until the church could fund my salary, but before we got to that date, I sensed God tell me, "Today is the day." I knew He meant it was the day to turn in my notice. I didn't want to. My salary at the bank gave us a comfortable living, and I didn't want to leave there and worry about what we were going to eat. (Great faith, huh?)

I told Tracy, and she didn't think it was God who spoke to me. I had to convince her it was.

That day, I went to see my boss, and I told him this was my notice because I was going to pastor the church full-time. I'll never forget his response. He said, "Chris, if anybody is called to be a pastor, it's you." He paused for a second, and then he said, "Let me ask you for one thing. If you ever want to go back into banking, call me first. We love you, and we'd love to have you back."

I appreciated his affirmation and kind offer. I asked, "Would you be willing to pay me for the next five weeks—salary, benefits, and 401K—to sow into me so I can do ministry?"

It was asking a lot, but he smiled. "Deal."

His generosity made the transition a little easier.

You don't get to carry the fire of God if you're not willing to carry the wood for the sacrifice. We often talk about "carrying our crosses" without thinking about what it means. The cross was an instrument of execution, and deaths were slow and painful. The condemned had to carry their crosses, and they were chaffed by the wood and stung by the splinters. Some people go into vocational ministry to be popular. They're disabused of that idea pretty soon when their sermons are critiqued and their leadership questioned. Ministry isn't about us; it's about Him. Paul wrote, "Therefore we make it our aim, whether present or absent, to be well pleasing to Him" (2 Corinthians 5:9). Aim is ambition. We often think ambition is a sin, but it depends on the purpose. If our hearts are fixed on personal popularity and gain, it's sin, but if our ambition—our heart's desire—is to please the One who bought us with a price, it's good, noble, and right.

You're Not Alone

You may be a single mom, a plumber, a business owner, a high school student, a retired grandparent, or any other kind of person on the face of the earth. Your stage of life and your career might be very different from others, but God is speaking to you, and He invites you to say, "Yes!" to a great adventure.

You're not alone in your quest. God has given us His Holy Spirit to lead us, comfort us, defend us from the enemy, and remind us that we're God's dear children. Listen to Him.

If you have a small group, even one or two close friends who are partners with you on this journey, treasure them. If you don't have people like that, find them. Look high and low, and don't quit until you find people who are committed to following God wherever He leads.

God spoke through Jeremiah that He has big plans for you, but remember, they're *His* plans, not yours. He often leads us into situations where we feel the full weight of our inadequacy. That's exactly where He wants us to be! Trust Him there. Be a doer of the Word, not just a hearer.

Whatever your stage of spiritual maturity, begin saying "Yes!" to God and keep saying "Yes!" to Him. Like I said at the beginning of this chapter, it's addictive . . . in a really good way!

I want to end the book by letting you know that Tracy and I have been covering this book and you in prayer. We've seen what saying, "Yes!" does in a person's life. No matter how you came across this book, whether it was a gift or a purchase, we've been praying that God would grab your heart, and those things you've been asked to launch, support, or serve will be fulfilled with your "Yes!"

Jeremiah 29:11 (NIV) reminds us, "'I know the plans that I have for you,'" declares the LORD . . ." How amazing is that? God has plans for you. The God who created the universe has plans for *you*!

The question is: Will you say "Yes"?

THINK ABOUT IT

CHAPTER 8

! Look at James 1:22. Who do you know who has developed the habit of saying "Yes!" to God and takes action? What impact does that person have on others? And on you?

! What are some ways God has been faithful to you?

! What are some symptoms of a "double mind"?

! Pick at least one and maybe more of the "maybe" statements in this chapter and write a prayer of how you want to respond to God:
- Experiencing God's love and forgiveness
- Rearranging your priorities around Him
- Repenting of recurring sins
- Inviting God to heal deep wounds
- Pulling the plug on comparison, competition, and resentment
- Doing "that thing" you've avoided
- Serving
- Answering God's call to vocational ministry

! Who are your partners on this journey? If you don't have them, how will you find them?

! What are some ways saying "Yes!" to God is addictive?

! What are two principles from this book you want to be sure to remember and apply?

USING *YES!!!* IN SMALL GROUPS AND CLASSES

This book is designed for individual study, small groups, and classes. The best way to absorb and apply these principles is for each person to individually study and answer the questions at the end of each chapter and then discuss them in a group environment. The chapters can also be taught in classes. The teacher can assign chapters to read and study before the class covers them.

Order enough copies of the book for each person to have a copy.

A recommended schedule for a small group or class might be:

Week 1: Introduce the material. As a group leader, tell your story of how your life changed when you developed the habit of saying "Yes!" to God. Share your hopes for the group, and provide books for each person. Encourage people to read the assigned chapter each week and answer the questions.

Weeks 2–9: Each week, introduce the topic for the week and share a story of how God has used the principles in your life. Lead people through a discussion of the questions at the end of the chapter.

Personalize Each Lesson.

Don't feel pressured to cover every question in your group discussions. You may have time for all of them, but if not, pick out three or four that had the biggest impact on you, and focus on those, or ask people in the group to share their responses to the questions that meant the most to them that week.

Make sure you personalize the principles and applications. At least once in each group meeting or class, add your own story to illustrate a particular point.

When you read a passage, make the Scriptures come alive. Far too often, we read the Bible like a phone book, with little or no emotion. Paint a vivid picture for people. Provide insights about the risk and the power of authentic relationships and help those in your group sense the emotions of specific people in each scene.

Focus on Application. The questions at the end of each chapter and your encouragement to group members to be authentic will help your group take big steps to apply the principles they're learning. Share how you are applying the principles in particular chapters each week, and encourage them to take steps of growth, too.

THREE TYPES OF QUESTIONS

If you've led groups for a few years, you already understand the importance of using open questions to stimulate discussion. Three types of questions are *limiting, leading,* and *open*. Many of the questions at the end of each lesson are open questions.

Limiting questions focus on an obvious answer, such as, "What does Jesus call Himself in John 10:11?" They don't stimulate reflection or discussion. If you want to use questions like these, follow them with thought-provoking, open questions.

Leading questions require the listener to guess what the leader has in mind, such as, "Why did Jesus use the metaphor of a shepherd in John 10?" (He was probably alluding to a passage in Ezekiel, but many people don't know that.) The teacher who asks a leading question has a definite answer in mind. Instead of asking this kind of question, you should just teach the point and perhaps ask an open question about the point you have made.

Open questions usually don't have right or wrong answers. They stimulate thinking, and they are far less threatening because the person answering doesn't risk ridicule for being wrong. These questions often begin with "Why do you think . . .?" or "What are some reasons that . . .?" or "How would you have felt in that situation?"

PREPARATION

As you prepare to teach this material in a group, consider these steps:

- **!** Carefully and thoughtfully read the book. Make notes, highlight key sections, quotes, or stories, and complete the reflection section at the end of each chapter. This will familiarize you with the entire scope of the content.

- **!** As you prepare for each week's group, read the corresponding chapter again and make additional notes.

- **!** Tailor the amount of content to the time allotted. You may not have time to cover all the questions, so pick the most relevant ones.

- **!** Add your own stories to personalize the message and add impact.

- **!** Before and during your preparation, ask God to give you wisdom, clarity, and power. Trust Him to use your group to change people's lives.

- **!** Most people will get far more out of the group if they read the chapter and complete the reflection each week. Order books before the group or class begins or after the first week.

ABOUT THE AUTHOR

Chris Binion is just a guy who continues to say, "YES!!!" to the Lord and has seen the Lord provide overwhelming opportunities. He is husband to Tracy, his wife of over thirty-five years, and father of two extremely gifted children who serve alongside him in ministry. He also has three incredible grandbabies he loves to love. Chris is an award-winning songwriter, comedian, and friend to pastors. He and Tracy co-founded Encounter Church in Fate, TX, now with three campuses and a fourth coming Fall 2026. They also co-founded The Pastor's Refuge, a non-profit offering pastors, spouses, and ministry leaders a place to rest and refocus so they can re-engage in healthy ministry. Because of his "YES!!!" to the Lord, he is now a published author.

RESOURCES

To contact Chris for a speaking request or church consultation connections, email him at

info@yourencounter.com.

For more information about *The Pastor's Refuge*, visit **ThePastorsRefuge.com**.

FOLLOW THE LEADER

STAY  CONNECTED

 facebook.com/TheArtofAvail   @theartofavail

△ AVAIL

LISTEN WHEREVER YOU GET YOUR PODCASTS
AVAIL LEADERSHIP PODCAST

www.ingramcontent.com/pod-product-compliance
Lightning Source LLC
Chambersburg PA
CBHW050900160426
43194CB00011B/2227